TOTAL CATECHESIS

Liturgy and the Sacraments

CATECHETICAL SESSIONS ON **Christian Morality**

Christian Prayer

the Creed

Pray It! Study It! Live It!™ resources offer a holistic approach
to learning, living, and passing on the Catholic faith.

The Total Faith™ Initiative

Total Catechesis

Catechetical Sessions on Christian Morality
Catechetical Sessions on Christian Prayer
Catechetical Sessions on Liturgy and the Sacraments
Catechetical Sessions on the Creed

Total Youth Ministry

Ministry Resources for Community Life
Ministry Resources for Evangelization
Ministry Resources for Justice and Service
Ministry Resources for Pastoral Care
Ministry Resources for Prayer and Worship
Ministry Resources for Youth Leadership Development

Total Faith™ Initiative Coordinator's Manual

The Catholic Faith Handbook for Youth

The Catholic Youth Bible™

TOTAL CATECHESIS

Liturgy and the Sacraments

CATECHETICAL SESSIONS ON **Christian Morality**

Christian Prayer

the Creed

Cheryl M. Tholcke with Eileen M. Daily and Steven C. McGlaun

Laurie Delgatto, general editor

Saint Mary's Press™

To my husband, Stephen:
Your love and support
make me a better person.

To my parents, Jim and Betty Stark:
You taught me what it means
to live a moral life.

Thanks to Stephen Tholcke, Jen Yearwood, and Tom East for sharing your insights with me on the topics covered in this book.

—Cheryl Tholcke

 Genuine recycled paper with 10% post-consumer waste. Printed with soy-based ink. 5085301

The publishing team included Eileen M. Daily, Laurie Delgatto, Steven C. McGlaun, and Barbara Murray, development editors; Lorraine Kilmartin, consultant and reviewer; Paul Grass, FSC, copy editor; Barbara Bartelson, production editor; Lynn Riska, typesetter; Cären Yang, art director and designer; Jonathan Thomas Goebel, cover design and illustrations on pages 103 and 167–168; Digital Images © PhotoDisc, Inc., cover images; Alan S. Hanson, prepress specialist; Elly Poppe, menus, interface, indexing, and CD; Benjamin Nagel, electronic scripting; Jim Koenig, multimedia and technical supervision; manufacturing coordinated by the production services department of Saint Mary's Press.

Printed in the United States of America

Printing: 9 8 7 6 5 4 3 2 1

Year: 2012 11 10 09 08 07 06 05 04

ISBN 0-88489-830-X

Contents

Introduction

The Total Faith™ Initiative: An Overview

In 1997 the United States Conference of Catholic Bishops (USCCB) published its blueprint for youth ministry in the twenty-first century. That document, *Renewing the Vision: A Framework for Catholic Youth Ministry,* highlights three goals for ministry with adolescents:

- to empower young people to live as disciples of Jesus Christ in our world today
- to draw young people to responsible participation in the life, mission, and work of the Catholic faith community
- to foster the total personal and spiritual growth of each young person

In *Renewing the Vision,* the bishops describe a rich and challenging vision for Catholic youth ministry. Catechesis is at the heart of that vision; throughout the document the bishops urge the Church to guide young people toward a life of fullness in Jesus Christ, and to give them the tools that will enable them to live out that fullness as Catholic Christians. To put it simply, the bishops call young people to embrace their faith as they study it, pray it, and live it. The bishops also challenge the faith community to surround young people with love, care, and attention and to include youth throughout the life of the parish.

By addressing each of the eight components for comprehensive youth ministry as articulated in *Renewing the Vision,* the TOTAL FAITH Initiative helps communities implement that vision. It addresses those elements in a way that pays attention to the intellectual, spiritual, and pastoral needs of young people. In this renewed vision, catechesis is one component of youth ministry; it is not distinct from it.

The initiative includes a three-part series that brings to the field of youth ministry the ancient yet timeless truths of the Catholic faith. The Scriptures and Tradition are set within a framework that any parish can apply in its everyday ministry with youth. From the initial proclamation of the Good News, through evangelization and outreach to effective catechesis,

The Pillars of the *Catechism* and Total Catechesis

Here is how the four parts, or pillars, of the *Catechism* and the Total Catechesis manuals are related:

- The first pillar of the *Catechism,* based on the Apostles' Creed, is covered in *Catechetical Sessions on the Creed.*
- The second pillar of the *Catechism,* based on the seven sacraments, is covered in *Catechetical Sessions on Liturgy and the Sacraments.*
- The third pillar of the *Catechism,* based on the Ten Commandments, is covered in *Catechetical Sessions on Christian Morality.*
- The fourth pillar of the *Catechism,* based on the Lord's Prayer, is covered in *Catechetical Sessions on Christian Prayer.*

In addition, the core text of the Total Catechesis series, *The Catholic Faith Handbook for Youth (CFH),* follows the same structure. The Ad Hoc Committee to Oversee the Use of the Catechism, United States Conference of Catholic Bishops, has found the *CFH* to be in conformity with the *Catechism.*

the TOTAL FAITH Initiative seeks to root youth in and connect them to the unchanging truths of their Catholic faith—while challenging them to apply the words of the Gospel and the teachings of Tradition to their daily lives. The TOTAL FAITH Initiative includes these components:

- ***The Catholic Faith Handbook for Youth (CFH)*** and the first edition of ***The Catholic Youth Bible (CYB)*** serve as the centerpieces of this initiative. Each book is an integrated resource for youth who are participating in the learning elements of the TOTAL FAITH Initiative.
- The **Total Youth Ministry** resource manuals address six of the components of youth ministry that are outlined in *Renewing the Vision.* The advocacy component, which is aimed primarily at the adult Church, is woven throughout the ministry resource manuals and is addressed specifically in the *TOTAL FAITH Initiative Coordinator's Manual.*
- The four catechetical manuals that comprise the **Total Catechesis** series are grounded in the content of the *CFH* and address the four pillars of the Catholic faith as outlined in the *Catechism of the Catholic Church.*

Total Catechesis: An Overview

Using tested strategies, catechists lead the participants through creative learning experiences and then invite them to reflect on those experiences. Prayer, the Scriptures, and other elements of Christian faith are carefully integrated into every manual in the series. These four manuals correspond to the four sections of the *CFH:*

- *Catechetical Sessions on Christian Morality*
- *Catechetical Sessions on Christian Prayer*
- *Catechetical Sessions on Liturgy and the Sacraments*
- *Catechetical Sessions on the Creed*

The manuals in the Total Catechesis series are Pray It! Study It! Live It!™ resources. The STUDY IT! component comprises a 45- to 60-minute core session focusing on the chapters found in the *CFH.* Optional activities, called session extensions, allow you to extend the core session to 90 minutes or longer. The PRAY IT! component offers a 10- to 15-minute prayer service on the session theme, and the LIVE IT! component suggests ways to connect the session topic to parish, community, and family life.

The Catholic Faith Handbook for Youth

The *CFH* is a teen's guide to the beliefs and practices of the Catholic Church. This book is an integrated text for youth who are participating in the learning elements of Total Catechesis. All the sessions in the Total Catechesis manuals are linked to this handbook. Leaders in youth ministry will also find it to be a helpful resource and guide for sharing and living the faith.

The Catholic Youth Bible

The *CYB* is designed for searchers and committed Christian youth to read and to apply the Scriptures to their life. The first edition of the *CYB* is linked to sessions throughout the Total Catechesis manuals and, therefore, is considered an important student resource.

An Added Feature: CD-ROMs

Each manual is accompanied by a CD-ROM containing the full content of its activities. This feature enables you to provide materials to catechists, adult leaders, parents, and young people in a variety of delivery methods, such as e-mail, Web site posting, and photocopying. Handouts and resources are provided in both color and black-and-white versions, and the latter can be customized for the particular needs of your group. Each CD-ROM also provides video clips, hyperlinks to suggested Web sites, and a selection from A Quiet Place Apart, a series of guided meditations from Saint Mary's Press.

Catechetical Sessions on Christian Morality: An Overview

Catechetical Sessions on Christian Morality is a rich course that gives young people a solid grounding in the foundations of Christian morality to add to what they have already received in their faith community and in their family. The manual presents young people with the fundamental concerns of the moral life in a Catholic Christian context. Above all, the course is an invitation to young people to build God's Reign by loving themselves and others as God loves them. In other words, *Catechetical Sessions on Christian Morality* is an invitation to become holy, healthy, and happy. In doing so, the young people will bring God and the world together!

Session Outcomes

Chapter 1: "Introduction to Christian Morality"

- The learner will be introduced to the Church's teaching on morality.
- The learner will understand the meaning in Catholic Tradition of beatitude, free will, and sin.
- The learner will realize that all humans are created in the image and likeness of God.
- The learner will apply the three factors for determining the morality of individual human actions: the action itself, the intent, and the circumstances.

Chapter 2: "Social Justice"

- The learner will recognize that God calls human society to reflect the loving relationship within the Trinity.
- The learner will understand the four foundations of Catholic social teaching: the common good, political responsibility, human dignity, and solidarity.
- The learner will discover the biblical roots of social justice.
- The learner will explore the interdependent relationship between service and justice.

Chapter 3: "Sources of Moral Truth"

- The learner will recognize natural law as part of human nature.
- The learner will appreciate the relationship between the Old Law (the Ten Commandments) and the New Law (the law of the Gospel).
- The learner will be able to identify the laws, or precepts, of the Church.
- The learner will discover ways to integrate these laws with the formation of conscience.

Chapter 4: "Honoring God"

- The learner will explore what it means to put God above all things.
- The learner will realize that everyday speech is a powerful tool for serving God.
- The learner will develop strategies for observing the Sabbath.

Chapter 5: "Honoring Family: An Intergenerational Session"

- The learner will appreciate that God is the source of the mutual respect due within the family.
- The learner will understand the relationship between the child's responsibility of respect and the parent's duty of care.
- The learner will understand how the fourth commandment applies to the civil authority.
- The learner will understand that civil disobedience and political action are based on Catholic teachings.

Chapter 6: "Respecting Life"

- The learner will recognize that the foundation of the fifth commandment is the fact that all humans are created in the image of God.
- The learner will understand how life issues—such as capital punishment, war, abortion, genetic engineering, euthanasia, suicide, and scandal—are related to the fifth commandment.

- The learner will realize that the responsibility to respect life includes respecting her or his own health.

Chapter 7: "Respecting Sexuality: The Gift of Sexuality"

- The learner will appreciate God's gift of sexuality.
- The learner will understand that marriage is the appropriate place for the full expression of the gift of sexuality.
- The learner will explore the value of chastity in marriage and in the single life.
- The learner will understand the reasons for the exclusive expression of sexual relations in a sacramental marriage, revealed in the sixth commandment, and the value of purity of heart, which is the basis of the ninth commandment.

Chapter 8: "Respecting Sexuality: The Challenge of Sexuality"

- The learner will understand how sexual sin separates us from God's plan and how chastity strengthens our relationship with God.
- The learner will confront the sexual temptations of today's culture, which affect both single and married people.
- The learner will understand the situation of the homosexual person in the context of God's gift of sexuality.

Chapter 9: "Respecting Material Goods"

- The learner will understand the Church's teaching on the seventh commandment with respect to stealing.
- The learner will be aware of the application of the tenth commandment to the dangers of materialism and envy.
- The learner will consider the best way to serve God through vocation, work, and wealth.

Chapter 10: "Respecting Truth"

- The learner will understand the importance of truth and the harm of lying.
- The learner will experience the power of words to make or break confidences and reputations.
- The learner will realize how important a foundation of truth is for society and how necessary reparations are when truth is violated.

Chapter 11: "The Moral Life"

- The learner will understand and learn how to cultivate the cardinal virtues: prudence, justice, temperance, and fortitude.
- The learner will understand the value and the source of the theological virtues: faith, hope, and charity.
- The learner will appreciate the meaning and importance of forgiveness and grace in living a Christian moral life.

How to Use This Manual

You may present the materials in this manual in its entirety, or you may select sessions and activities that you think will be best for the young people with whom you work. The sessions and activities are not sequential, so you may organize them in the way that is most appropriate for your situation.

Each session begins with a brief overview, a list of expected outcomes, and a list of recommended background reading that includes corresponding *CFH* pages, related *Catechism* paragraphs, scriptural connections, and *CYB* article connections. All articles are excerpted from the first edition of the *CYB*. The next element is a suggested schedule, which is to be used as a starting point and modified according to your circumstances. A checklist of the preparation required, including all materials needed, is the next part of the presentation of every session. A complete description of the session procedure is then provided, including a core activity, session extensions, prayer experiences, and options and actions. The procedure descriptions are formatted as follows.

STUDY IT! A Core Session and Session Extensions

Each session can be expanded and customized to meet your schedule and the needs of your group. All the sessions begin with a core activity that should be used before any other activity in the session plan. Core sessions are structured for a 40- to 45-minute time frame and correspond to the content in the *CFH*. You may expand the sessions by using additional activities known as session extensions. These strategies vary in length from 10 to 60 minutes. Session extensions are intended for further development and study of the session theme and topics.

All the learning strategies in this manual are based on the praxis method of experience, analysis, and reflection, in dialogue with the Scriptures and Tradition, leading to synthesis of new learnings and insights. Variations are often suggested, including ideas for gender-specific groups and for larger or smaller groups.

Some manuals include sidebars that suggest specific *CFH* connections, and all manuals incorporate sidebars that suggest specific musical selections from *Spirit & Song* (Portland, OR: OCP Publications, 1999). The lists in those sidebars are not exhaustive; music resources are available from a variety of music publishers, and a Bible concordance will provide additional citations if you want to add a more substantial scriptural component to a session. *The Saint Mary's Press Essential Bible Concordance* offers a simple, user-friendly index to key words in the Bible. Some of the sessions provide a list of media resources—such as print, video, and Internet—for more exploration. Family approaches provide simple, follow-up suggestions for family learning, enrichment, celebration, prayer, and service. In addition, all the activities can be enhanced by the creativity and expertise of the adult leader.

Because catechesis requires personal reflection, a Journal Activities sidebar with questions and suggestions for deeper analysis and reflection is provided in most sessions. Although those questions and suggestions may be used for oral discussion, it is recommended that they be employed to prompt a written exercise. An ongoing journal, reflection papers, or letters to themselves or God can help the participants process the material and activities, making connections to their own lives.

Pray It! Prayer Experiences

Each session includes opportunities and suggestions for prayer focused on the session's theme. Prayer forms include guided meditation, shared prayer, music, silence, prayers by young people, reflective reading, and experiences created by the participants. The Pray It! component gives the young people an opportunity to bring their insights and concerns to God in prayer. The time frame for prayer experiences varies from 5 to 20 minutes.

Live It! Options and Actions

This manual can be a springboard for connections with other youth ministry experiences. Therefore all its sessions include additional strategies to support the learning process. Those activities provide good follow-up for the Study It! core activities, and allow for age-appropriate assimilation of the material. They might include off-site events, intergenerational ideas, parish involvement, prayer and liturgical celebrations, service options, and social action.

Session Talk Points

To encourage and support the growth of family faith, each session offers a "take home" handout that presents talk points, to encourage ongoing conversation about the session's topics. The handout includes a summary of the session content, which is taken directly from the corresponding chapter of the *CFH*. Participants can also use the handout with small community groups, with peer groups, and for personal reflection. With this material available on a CD-ROM, you can customize it and choose a means of delivery that works best for your situation.

Handouts and Resources

All the necessary handouts and resources for a session are found at the end of that session in the manual. They are also found on the accompanying CD-ROM, in both color and black-and-white versions. The black-and-white materials may be customized to suit your particular needs.

Teaching This Course

Preparing Yourself

Read each session or activity before you facilitate it; then use it creatively to meet the needs of the young people in your group. Knowing your audience will help you determine which strategies will work best for it. Some of the activities require preparation. Allow yourself adequate time to get ready.

All the sessions include presentations of key concepts and teachings. The session plans offer guidelines for these talks. Preparing for those presentations is vital to the success of each session. You will want to review relevant content in the *CFH* and the *Catechism.* Spend time putting these presentations together so that they are clear and hold the attention of the participants.

Standard Materials

To save time, consider gathering frequently used materials in bins and storing those bins in a place that is accessible to all staff and volunteer leaders. Here are some recommendations for organizing the bins.

Supply Bin

The following items appear frequently in the materials checklists:

- *The Catholic Youth Bible,* at least one for every two participants
- *The Catholic Faith Handbook for Youth,* at least one for every two participants
- masking tape
- cellophane tape
- washable and permanent markers (thick-line and thin-line)
- pens or pencils
- self-stick notes
- scissors
- newsprint

- blank paper, scrap paper, and notebook paper
- journals, one for each participant
- index cards
- baskets
- candles and matches
- items to create a prayer space (for example, a colored cloth, a cross, a bowl for water, and a vase for flowers)

Music Bin

Young people often find profound meaning in the music and lyrics of songs, both past and present. Also, the right music can set the appropriate mood for a prayer or an activity. Begin with a small collection of tapes or CDs in a music bin, and add to it over time. You might ask the young people to put some of their favorite music in the bin. The bin might include the following styles of music:

- *Prayerful, reflective instrumental music,* such as the kind that is available in the adult alternative section of music stores. Labels that specialize in this type of music include Windham Hill and Narada.
- *Popular songs with powerful messages.* If you are not well versed in popular music, ask the young people to offer suggestions.
- *The music of contemporary Catholic artists.* Many young people are familiar with the work of Catholic musicians such as Steve Angrisano, Sarah Hart, David W. Kauffman, Michael Mahler, Jesse Manibusan, and Danielle Rose.

Also consider including songbooks and hymnals. Many of the musical selections suggested in Total Catechesis are taken from the *Spirit & Song* hymnal, published by Oregon Catholic Press (OCP). If you wish to order copies of this hymnal, please contact OCP directly at *www.ocp.org* or by calling 800-548-8749. Including copies of your parish's chosen hymnal is a suitable option as well. You might also check with your liturgy or music director for recordings of parish hymns.

Some Closing Thoughts

As a catechist you have taken on an exciting and profoundly important task. We hope you find this material helpful as you invite young people into a deeper relationship with the marvelous community of faith we know as the Catholic Church. Please be assured of our continual prayers for you and the young people you serve.

Your Comments or Suggestions

Saint Mary's Press wants to know your reactions to the materials in the Total Catechesis series. We are open to all kinds of suggestions, including these:

- an alternative way to conduct an activity
- an audiovisual or other media resource that worked well with this material
- a book or an article you found helpful
- an original activity or process
- a prayer experience or service
- a helpful preparation for other leaders
- an observation about the themes or content of this material

If you have a comment or suggestion, please write to us at 702 Terrace Heights, Winona, MN 55987-1318; call us at our toll-free number, 800-533-8095; or e-mail us at *smp@smp.org*. Your ideas will help improve future editions of Total Catechesis.

Introduction to Christian Morality

AT A GLANCE

Study It

Core Session

◆ What Makes an Action Moral?
(45 minutes)

Session Extensions

◆ Created in the Image and Likeness of God
(20 minutes)
◆ Hometown Heroes
(25 minutes)

Pray It

◆ Called to God
(15 minutes)

Live It

◆ The good Samaritan for today
◆ Maturity checklist
◆ Bound to goodness
◆ An apple a day
◆ Sin inside and out

Overview

Young people are more likely to be open to the challenges of living a moral life if they first understand its relationship to their free will, their happiness or beatitude, and their creation in the image of God. This introductory session on Christian morality covers the foundational concepts that underlie Christian morality in the Catholic context. The session also addresses sin in its multiple forms and the effect of sin on a person's relationship with God. Participants will learn a framework for assessing the morality of their actions.

Outcomes

◆ The learner will be introduced to the Church's teaching on morality.
◆ The learner will understand the meaning in Catholic Tradition of beatitude, free will, and sin.
◆ The learner will realize that all humans are created in the image and likeness of God.
◆ The learner will apply the three factors for determining the morality of individual human actions: the action itself, the intent, and the circumstances.

Background Reading

◆ This session covers pages 206–215 of *The Catholic Faith Handbook for Youth.*
◆ For further exploration, check out paragraph numbers 1691–1761 and 1846–1876 of the *Catechism.*
◆ Scriptural connections: Gen. 1:26–31 (Creation), Matt. 5:1–12 (the Beatitudes), Luke 10:25–37 (the good Samaritan)

◆ *Catholic Youth Bible* article connections: "In God's Image" (Gen. 1:26–27), "An Upside-Down Kingdom" (Matt. 5:1–12), "A Top-Shelf Life" (Col. 3:1–4)

Study it!

Core Session

What Makes an Action Moral? (45 minutes)

Preparation

* Gather the following items:
  - ❑ copies of handout 1, "Introduction to Christian Morality," one for each participant
  - ❑ copies of handout 2, "Morally Good or Morally Suspect?" one for each small group
  - ❑ pens
  - ❑ newsprint
  - ❑ masking tape
  - ❑ markers
* Review the summary points in step 1 of this session and the relevant material on pages 206–215 of *The Catholic Faith Handbook for Youth (CFH)*. Be prepared to share the information with the young people.
* Create three newsprint sheets for the participants to view during the exercise:
  - ○ The first sheet has the heading "Action" and displays these questions: Does this action promote well-being for me and for others? Does the action show respect for God, for me, and for others?
  - ○ The second sheet has the heading "Intent" and displays these questions: What do you hope to accomplish by making this choice? What is the underlying "good" you are trying to achieve? Does that "good" reflect what God wants for you?
  - ○ The third sheet has the heading "Circumstances" and displays these questions: What influences are causing you to consider this action? How free are you to choose not to do it?

  1. Begin the session by conducting a brief presentation on Christian morality, using the bullet points below, which are taken from pages 206–215 of the *CFH:*

Mediaconnections

◆ Invite the participants to watch an episode of *The Andy Griffith Show, Leave It to Beaver,* or *Little House on the Prairie.* Although people might laugh at the way the characters dress or how old-fashioned they appear when compared with today's TV sitcoms, moral stories happen in each episode. Offer these questions for discussion: What happened to the characters? What was the situation? What choices were possible? What choice was made? What moral lesson does the episode convey?

◆ Suggest that as the participants watch television this week, they look for the moral lesson in the shows they view. Although the characters might not be acting morally, invite the participants to consider this question: If I were re-writing this show to

- When we venture into the territory of deciding between right and wrong, we are talking about morality, "the goodness or evil of human acts" (*CCC*, p. 888).

- God's gift of free will means that we have the ability to make conscious choices.

- So our question is, "How do we live the right way?"—which for Catholics means "How does God want me to live?" Fortunately we have the Scriptures and Tradition to help answer that question. WWSD/WWGW

- From the moment you were conceived, you were made in God's image, meaning that you—and every other person on earth—are first and foremost essentially good. When we choose wisely, we are acting in accordance with our true nature. This is why doing the right thing ultimately makes us happy.

- Our source of happiness is not material success, fame, or unending hours of leisure and pleasure. Rather, what God intends for us is complete joy and a sense of well-being. Our ultimate destiny is to be eternally happy with God in heaven. Jesus gives us a glimpse of this destiny in the Beatitudes (Matt. 5:3–12 and Luke 6:20–26). *Beatitude* means "perfect happiness or blessedness."

- God created us in his image with a natural desire to follow the moral law, to do good and avoid evil. At the same time, because of original sin, we are inclined toward sin, or choosing to do the wrong thing. The ability to use reason to distinguish between right and wrong is the work of our conscience. Our conscience is the interior voice that helps us to know right from wrong and then to act on that knowledge.

- But that's where our free will comes in. We can consciously choose the truly good life. Of course, this gift of human freedom has a flip side. We are also responsible for the choices we make.

- Three factors determine the morality of any human action: (1) whether the action itself is inherently good or evil, (2) the intention of the person doing the action, and (3) the circumstances of the action. All three of these elements help determine whether a particular act is good or bad.

- When we choose to do wrong instead of doing good, we commit sin, and we hurt our relationship with our self, with others, and with God. Sin is any word that we speak, action that we perform, or desire that we have that is contrary to the law that God has inscribed in our heart at the very moment we are conceived.

- Christian morality, then, is being the person God created you to be—a person who chooses to be good. You grow into a moral person by choosing good acts, carefully examining your motives to be sure your intentions are good, and avoiding circumstances that lessen your ability to choose freely.

reflect Catholic morality, what would I change?

◆ Suggest that when the participants hear a favorite song this week, they concentrate on the message it proclaims. Whether it is a love song or something else, ask them to consider the following questions: Does the song's message convey a moral value? If yes, what is that moral value? If no, what moral value does it contradict? Why would you spend your time listening to something that is not in keeping with your Catholic morality?

TryThis

Instead of or in addition to using the questions on handout 2, have the participants identify some of the moral dilemmas they face in life. Perform the "action–intent–circumstances" analysis with these situations.

2. Distribute pens and divide the participants into groups of two to four. Tape the newsprint sheets on the wall. Give each group a copy of handout 2.

3. Describe the exercise to the participants as follows:
- The goal is to explore whether particular activities are moral or not, based on an analysis of the three factors that determine the morality of any human action: the action itself, the intent, and the circumstances.
- Handout 2 presents a series of moral dilemmas. You have an opportunity to decide whether the action is good, neutral, or bad; whether the intent is good; and whether any circumstances limit the freedom to decide.
- The questions on the newsprint will help you make these determinations.

4. Give the groups 15 minutes to complete the handout. Consider walking through the first question to set an example of how the participants will need to proceed. Remind them when necessary to look at the questions on the newsprint.

5. When the groups have completed the handout, discuss each question in order. If the groups don't agree on the analysis of a particular situation, talk through the differences. Then have the whole group determine whether the person should do the act. Consider asking the participants for alternative actions if they determine that the person should not do the act. Then discuss those options as well. Refer to the questions on the newsprint as necessary. If participants are having trouble making a decision, explain again that the action must be good or neutral, the intent must be good, and the circumstances must not impair the freedom of the person deciding. Point out how these conditions have or have not been met.

6. Close this activity by inviting the participants to apply this analysis tool to the decisions they have to make this week. Be sure to note that the content of this session was drawn from chapter 21 of the *CFH*. Encourage the participants to read and review it in the next few days.

Session Extensions

Created in the Image and Likeness of God (20 minutes)

Preparation
- Gather the following items:
  - ❑ modeling clay, a piece that fills the palm of the hand, one piece for each participant
  - ❑ newsprint
  - ❑ markers

❏ a tape player or a CD player

❏ instrumental music

- Write the following quotes on separate sheets of newsprint:
  - Of all earthly creatures, only man is "capable of knowing and loving his Creator" (*Gaudium et Spes*, no. 12).
  - "Being in the image of God the human individual possesses the dignity of a person, who is not just something, but someone. . . . And he is called by grace to a covenant with his Creator, to offer him a response of faith and love that no other creature can give in his stead" (*CCC*, no. 357).
  - "God created everything for man,[1] but man in turn was created to serve and love God and to offer all creation back to him" (*CCC*, no. 358).
  - "So God created humankind in his image,
    in the image of God he created them;
    male and female he created them" (Gen. 1:27).

1. Introduce this activity by saying something like the following:
- We have always heard that we are created in the image and likeness of God. Often we find that hard to believe. We do not have perfect features; we are not always as nice as we should be, and the list goes on. So how can we be created in God's image?

  Read Genesis 1:27.

2. Distribute a piece of modeling clay to each participant. Give these directions, taking your time, pausing after each bullet point, and using a gentle, low voice:
- Close your eyes, or look at a neutral spot that won't distract you. Do not look at the clay. Allow yourself to get comfortable.
- Think about the fact that you are created in the image and likeness of God.
- Feel the clay in your hands. Without looking at it, move it around, squish it, squeeze it, shape it, mold it, and squish it again. Keep manipulating the clay, paying attention to how it feels, letting yourself get used to having it in your hands.
- While you are still working the clay in your hands, think again about being made in the image of God. What does this statement mean to you? For what godly qualities are you especially grateful? What might you be able to do someday with these qualities?
- Now stop working the clay, and open your eyes. Look at the clay in your hands. Does it look like anything in particular? Take a moment to make any small changes in it, but leave it mostly as it is.
- Can you see whether what you have created in the clay represents who you are as a person created in the image of God? Does your clay figure reflect a current mood?

JournalACTIVITIES

◆ How does living a moral life help me grow into the person God intends me to become?

◆ What did I do this week to exercise *free will* in favor of God, to avoid *sin*, and to live a life of *beatitude*? What did I do that worked against exercising *free will* in favor of God, avoiding *sin*, and living a life of *beatitude*?

◆ Read these words from Pope John Paul II at the beginning of the day, and keep them in mind throughout the day. At the end of the day, answer this question: How did I see this wisdom come to life today?

To be truly free does not at all mean doing everything that pleases me, or doing what I want to do. . . . To be truly free means to use one's own freedom for what is a true good.

(Pope John Paul II, *Dilecti Amici*, quoted in *CFH*, p. 209)

Draw attention to and incorporate in your remarks the quotes that you have posted on newsprint. Invite discussion by asking questions like the following to draw the participants deeper into the quotations:

- What does the first quote suggest about your responsibility to God? Is your responsibility different than that of other creatures? Why?
- This question leads to the second quote, which uses the word *dignity*. What does dignity mean to you in this context? Think about yourself in relationship to God. Does this thought shift your self-perception at all? Do you see dignity in yourself?
- Do you ever forget that all creation, including you, is a gift from God? What can you do to remind yourself of this fact?
- What does it mean to you that God created male and female in God's image? Is each man or each woman in God's image or is their combination in God's image?
- What are the implications of the answers to these questions for the way you live?

Allow 5 to 10 minutes for completion. Consider playing instrumental music while the participants are working with the clay.

3. Invite the participants to describe to a partner how their individual clay sculpture represents the reflection of God they see within themselves.

Hometown Heroes (25 minutes)

Preparation

- Gather the following items:
  - ❏ copies of handout 3, "A Hometown Hero," one for each participant
  - ❏ pens or pencils
  - ❏ newsprint
  - ❏ markers

1. Invite the participants to find a partner. Distribute a copy of handout 3 and a pen or a pencil to each participant.

2. Set up the scenario by offering the following explanation:

- The hometown newspaper offers a regular feature called "Hometown Heroes," which highlights some of the town's noteworthy citizens. They are not necessarily famous, just people who are trying their best to live a good life. Some of them still live in town; others live elsewhere.
- Imagine that it is twenty years from today and that the newspaper has selected you as a subject for the next article on hometown heroes.
- Partners are to interview each other by using the handout provided. When your partner answers a question, write the response in the space provided on the handout. You will have about 5 minutes for each interview.

TryThis

If your group is small enough or if you have enough time, invite the pairs of participants from step 3 to introduce each other to the whole group and to describe what they molded with their clay.

3. Ask the pairs to exchange handouts so that all participants have their own responses. Then conduct a brief presentation on the meaning of *beatitude,* using the bullet points below, which are taken from pages 207–209 of the *CFH:*

- The foundation of morality, of doing the right thing, is found in the first chapter of Genesis. From the moment you were conceived, you were made in God's image, meaning that you—and every other person on earth—are first and foremost essentially good. When we choose wisely, we are acting in accordance with our true nature. This is why doing the right thing ultimately makes us happy.
- Happiness is not determined by what we normally see in magazines, on television, or in the movies. Our source of happiness is not material success, fame, or unending hours of leisure and pleasure. Rather, what God intends for us is complete joy and a sense of well-being. Our ultimate destiny is to be eternally happy with God in heaven.
- *Beatitude* means "perfect happiness or blessedness."
- Being made in God's image does not make us perfect; God gave us a soul, intellect, and free will to make our own choices. Although God wants each of us to be part of the Kingdom that Jesus spoke about, free will means that we have the freedom to accept or reject God's will.
- God created us in his image with a natural desire to follow the moral law, to do good and avoid evil.

4. Have the participants respond to the presentation by brainstorming the ways a person can live *a life of beatitude.* Record their suggestions on a sheet of newsprint.

5. Ask them to review their responses to the questions that the Hometown Hero interviewer asked them. Invite them to compare their Hometown Hero answers with the ones just written on newsprint, with respect to what it means to *live a life of beatitude.* Then ask:

- Does the person you would like to be twenty years from now, as represented on your handout, look like someone who is *living a life of beatitude?*

6. Ask the participants to think again about what kind of person they will be in twenty years. Then pose the following question:

- Would you add or change anything in your interview to reflect your commitment to exercise *free will* in favor of God, to avoid *sin,* and to live a life of *beatitude?*

Allow time for the pairs to share their responses to this question.

(This activity is adapted from Marilyn Kielbasa, *Called to Live the Gospel,* pp. 23–24.)

Familyconnections

- Invite the participants to engage their mom, dad, or guardian in a conversation about their favorite music while growing up. What kinds of values did those songs address? Did the older generation listen to music that supported their Catholic values? How has music changed over the years?
- Invite participants and their families to talk about how their family tries to experience perfect happiness or blessedness, the beatitude that God calls them to share with him.
- Invite participants and their families to talk about the virtues that might help them overcome temptations to commit the seven deadly sins: pride, avarice (greed), envy, wrath, lust, gluttony, and sloth.
- Suggest a family discussion about why owning up to sin is so hard to do. Why do people blame some person or influence other than themselves when they do something wrong? What makes it so hard to admit that we made the wrong choice?

Spirit & Song connections

- "Christ, Be Our Light," by Bernadette Farrell
- "Lead Me, Lord," by John D. Becker
- "Holy Spirit," by Ken Canedo

Called to God (15 minutes)

Preparation

- Gather the following items:
  - ❑ a Paschal candle
  - ❑ a tape player or a CD player
  - ❑ instrumental music
  - ❑ copies of resource 1, "Examination of Conscience," one for each of the six volunteer readers
- Ask for six volunteers, each to read one of the statements on resource 1, "Examination of Conscience."

   1. With instrumental music playing in the background, gather the participants in a circle around the lit Paschal candle. Say something like the following:

- As we close our time together, I invite you to center yourself and to focus on your relationship with God. We have spent some time talking and reflecting on the Church's teaching regarding morality.
- We know that morality affects every aspect of our life. God calls each of us to holiness and happiness. Living a moral life brings us closer to God and to holiness and happiness.
- God's love is written on our heart; God's love gives us the strength to do good and to avoid evil.
- In the Letter to the Ephesians, Saint Paul offers this prayer on our behalf:

   > May God "grant that you may be strengthened in your inner being with power through his Spirit, and that Christ may dwell in your hearts through faith." (3:16–17)

- Let us now turn our attention to a brief examination of conscience.
- The Paschal candle in our midst is a symbol of Christ, the light in our life, the one who leads us to God. At times, however, we step away from the light; at times our free choices pull us away from God, away from the light of Christ.

   2. Have each of the six volunteers read, in order, one of the following statements from resource 1:

- For the times when I did not take care of myself; when the choices I made brought harm to my body, my mind, and my soul; and when I suffered because of my thoughts, words, or actions. *[Everyone takes a step or two back from the Paschal candle while continuing to face the candle.]*
- For the times when I hurt another person—a friend, a brother or a sister, a parent, a classmate, or a stranger on the street—or when I harmed my relationship with another person by my thoughts, words, or actions. *[Everyone takes a step or two back from the Paschal candle.]*
- For the times when I turned away from God, from the light of his Son, Jesus, and when my thoughts, words, and actions kept me from growing in my relationship with God. *[Everyone turns around and faces away from the Paschal candle.]*

The leader says the following:

- All is not lost; we can and do make choices to turn back toward the light.

The volunteers continue reading:

- For the times when I turned to God for help and to give thanks and praise for the blessings in my life, and when I tried to live a life in the manner of Jesus. *[Everyone turns back toward the candle and takes a step forward.]*
- For the times when I was a good friend or son or daughter and when I reached out to another person in love and compassion. *[Everyone takes a step or two forward.]*
- For the times when I made good decisions about myself and my life and when I said yes to becoming the person God created me to be. *[Everyone takes a step or two forward.]*

3. When the group is clustered tightly around the Paschal candle, invite the participants to raise their hands in a blessing to one another. Say the following prayer or something similar:

- O God, you have fashioned us in your image and likeness. We recognize the goodness in one another and in ourselves. Bless us as we strive to live a holy, happy, and healthy life as your Son taught us. Keep us safe from harm, and help us as we struggle to live a moral life. We ask this in the name of your Son, Jesus. Amen.

Options and Actions

- **The good Samaritan for today.** Reflect on the painting of the parable of the good Samaritan on page 208 of the *CFH,* and read the parable in Luke (10:25–37). Compose a children's book about the parable of the good Samaritan, using places and people that young children can recognize.

- **Maturity checklist.** Invite the participants to brainstorm the qualities that a mature person might possess. Some examples are the capacity to accept failure, the ability to draw out the best in people, a sense of humor, and the acceptance of personal responsibility. See whether the group can suggest at least twenty-five qualities. Using this list, create a maturity inventory that allows the participants to rate themselves on how far along they are in developing these qualities (adapted from Marilyn Kielbasa, *Called to Live the Gospel,* p. 24).

- **Bound to goodness.** Provide the participants with three different colors of embroidery thread to represent happiness with God, free will, and good moral choices. Invite them to create a bracelet or anklet by braiding the three pieces of thread to wear as a reminder of the need to turn toward God and away from sin.

- **An apple a day.** Toss an apple around the group. The first participant who catches the apple gives an example of one way a person is tempted to sin; the next person who catches the apple describes a way to avoid or resist that temptation. Give all the participants an apple to take home, and suggest that they conduct this activity with their family members.

- **Sin inside and out.** Provide each participant with a large white envelope. Invite everyone to glue pictures or words on the outside of the envelope to represent the attractive things that entice people into foolish and sinful ways. Then ask them to glue pictures or words on sheets of paper to show the evil that lurks behind those false appearances. Have them stuff the sheets into the envelopes.

Introduction to Christian Morality

This session covers pages 206–215 of *The Catholic Faith Handbook for Youth*. For further exploration, check out paragraph numbers 1691–1761 and 1846–1876 of the *Catechism of the Catholic Church*.

Session Summary

- When we venture into the territory of deciding between right and wrong, we are talking about morality, "the goodness or evil of human acts" (*CCC*, page 888).
- God's gift of free will means that we have the ability to make conscious choices.
- So our question is, "How do we live the right way?" which for Catholics means, "How does God want me to live?" Fortunately we have the Scriptures and Tradition to help answer that question.
- The foundation of morality, of doing the right thing, is found in the first chapter of Genesis. From the moment you were conceived, you were made in God's image, meaning that you—and every other person on earth—are first and foremost essentially good. When we choose wisely, we are acting in accordance with our true nature. This is why doing the right thing ultimately makes us happy.
- Happiness is not determined by what we normally see in magazines, on television, or in the movies.
- Our source of happiness is not material success, fame, or unending hours of leisure and pleasure. Rather, what God intends for us is complete joy and a sense of well-being. Our ultimate destiny is to be eternally happy with God in heaven. Jesus gives us a glimpse of this destiny in the Beatitudes (Matthew 5:3–12 and Luke 6:20–26, NRSV). *Beatitude* means "perfect happiness or blessedness."
- Being made in God's image does not make us perfect; God gave us a soul, intellect, and free will to make our own choices. Although God wants each of us to be part of the Kingdom that Jesus spoke about, free will means that we have the freedom to accept or reject God's will.
- God created us in his image with a natural desire to follow the moral law, to do good and avoid evil. At the same time, because of original sin, we are inclined toward sin, or choosing to do the wrong thing. The ability to

use reason to distinguish between right and wrong is the work of our conscience. Our conscience is the interior voice that helps us to know right from wrong and then to act on that knowledge.

- But that's where our free will comes in. We can consciously choose the truly good life. Of course, this gift of human freedom has a flip side. We are also responsible for the choices we make.
- Three factors determine the morality of any human action: (1) whether the action itself is inherently good or evil, (2) the intention of the person doing the action, and (3) the circumstances of the action. All three of these elements help determine whether a particular act is good or bad.
- When we choose to do wrong instead of doing good, we commit sin, and we hurt our relationship with our self, with others, and with God. Sin is any word that we speak, action that we perform, or desire that we have that is contrary to the law that God has inscribed in our heart at the very moment we are conceived.
- Christian morality, then, is being the person God created you to be—a person who chooses to be good. You grow into a moral person by choosing good acts, carefully examining your motives to be sure your intentions are good, and avoiding circumstances that lessen your ability to choose freely.

(The summary point labeled *CCC* is from the *Catechism of the Catholic Church* for use in the United States of America, page 888. Copyright © 1994 by the United States Catholic Conference, Inc.—Libreria Editrice Vaticana. Used with permission.)

(All summary points are taken from *The Catholic Faith Handbook for Youth,* by Brian Singer-Towns et al. [Winona, MN: Saint Mary's Press, 2004], pages 206–215. Copyright © 2004 by Saint Mary's Press. All rights reserved.)

Talk Points

- What are some of the most difficult moral issues that you face? (*CFH,* p. 215)
- How does studying and talking about morality help you to be more aware of right and wrong? Why is it important to have these discussions with other faith-filled Catholics? (*CFH,* p. 215)
- Name something that you keep doing wrong, even though you are trying to do better. Write a letter to yourself that encourages you to keep on trying and suggests a different strategy for overcoming the obstacle.
- Read a biography about someone you admire, or interview an adult whom you respect. Then write about the acts, habits, and character of that person.

Morally Good or Morally Suspect?

For each situation, determine whether the action itself is good, neutral, or bad; whether the intent is good; and whether the circumstances keep the person who is considering the action from acting freely.

1. You are wondering whether to attend a party at a friend's house this weekend. Everyone in the school knows that no parents will be present.

Action itself: _____ Good _____ Neutral _____ Wrong

Intent: _____ Good _____ Not good

Circumstances: _____ Free to decide _____ Not free to decide

2. Because you haven't had time to write your paper and it is late, you are wondering whether to download a paper from the Internet to hand in tomorrow as your own.

Action itself: _____ Good _____ Neutral _____ Wrong

Intent: _____ Good _____ Not good

Circumstances: _____ Free to decide _____ Not free to decide

3. Although you have been going out exclusively with the same person for two months, you are wondering if it is okay to take a walk with a new kid at school.

Action itself: _____ Good _____ Neutral _____ Wrong

Intent: _____ Good _____ Not good

Circumstances: _____ Free to decide _____ Not free to decide

4. Because your parents need you to baby-sit, you are wondering if you should call in sick at work on Friday night.

Action itself: _____ Good _____ Neutral _____ Wrong

Intent: _____ Good _____ Not good

Circumstances: _____ Free to decide _____ Not free to decide

5. Because you don't want any part in such an activity, you are wondering whether to lie to your friend who is asking you to come with him to pick up a bag of marijuana.

Action itself: _____ Good _____ Neutral _____ Wrong

Intent: _____ Good _____ Not good

Circumstances: _____ Free to decide _____ Not free to decide

6. Because you don't want anyone at school to know that your mother is away for a month and that the housekeeper is the only adult living in the house with you, you are wondering whether to sign your mother's name on a permission slip.

Action itself: _____ Good _____ Neutral _____ Wrong

Intent: _____ Good _____ Not good

Circumstances: _____ Free to decide _____ Not free to decide

7. Because a friend of yours has been talking about suicide and is not answering the cell phone, you are wondering whether to take the family car and drive over to your friend's house, even though you don't have any way right now to contact your parents and ask for permission to use the car.

Action itself: _____ Good _____ Neutral _____ Wrong

Intent: _____ Good _____ Not good

Circumstances: _____ Free to decide _____ Not free to decide

8. Because you know that someone is going to be at the party whom you are not allowed to, or don't want to, hang out with, you are wondering whether to tell your friend that you won't be coming to her party Saturday night.

Action itself: _____ Good _____ Neutral _____ Wrong

Intent: _____ Good _____ Not good

Circumstances: _____ Free to decide _____ Not free to decide

9. You are wondering whether to tell a counselor a secret that you promised your best friend you wouldn't reveal: that your friend is binging and purging a couple of times a day.

Action itself: _____ Good _____ Neutral _____ Wrong

Intent: _____ Good _____ Not good

Circumstances: _____ Free to decide _____ Not free to decide

10. You are wondering whether to make a copy of a note that you saw at work in a local market. Because the manager heard a rumor that your father is passing bad checks, the note tells cashiers not to accept any checks from him. You know that he is honest.

Action itself: _____ Good _____ Neutral _____ Wrong

Intent: _____ Good _____ Not good

Circumstances: _____ Free to decide _____ Not free to decide

A Hometown Hero

Where do you live?

What kind of work do you do?

Tell me about your family.

What do you like to do?

In what activities are you involved?

What or who has been the greatest influence on your life?

In what ways do you make a difference in the life of others?

Of what are you proud?

At what do you want to get better?

What three words or phrases would you use to describe yourself?

(This handout is adapted from *Called to Live the Gospel,* by Marilyn Kielbasa [Winona, MN: Saint Mary's Press, 2000], page 30. Copyright © 2000 by Saint Mary's Press. All rights reserved.)

Examination of Conscience

Each of the six volunteers reads one of the following statements:

- For the times when I did not take care of myself; when the choices I made brought harm to my body, my mind, and my soul; and when I suffered because of my thoughts, words, or actions. *[Everyone takes a step or two back from the Paschal candle while continuing to face the candle.]*

- For the times when I hurt another person—a friend, a brother or a sister, a parent, a classmate, or a stranger on the street—or when I harmed my relationship with another person by my thoughts, words, or actions. *[Everyone takes a step or two back from the Paschal candle.]*

- For the times when I turned away from God, from the light of his Son, Jesus, and when my thoughts, words, and actions kept me from growing in my relationship with God. *[Everyone turns around, facing away from the Paschal candle.]*

The leader says the following:

- All is not lost; we can and do make choices to turn back toward the light.

The volunteers continue reading:

- For the times when I turned to God for help and to give thanks and praise for the blessings in my life, and when I tried to live a life in the manner of Jesus. *[Everyone turns back toward the candle and takes a step forward.]*

- For the times when I was a good friend or son or daughter and when I reached out to another person in love and compassion. *[Everyone takes a step or two forward.]*

- For the times when I made good decisions about myself and my life and when I said yes to becoming the person God created me to be. *[Everyone takes a step or two forward.]*

2 Social Justice

AT A GLANCE

Study It

Core Session

◆ Catholic Social Teaching
(45 minutes)

Session Extensions

◆ The Social Justice Two-
Step
(15 minutes)

◆ We Lift It Up to You,
Lord
(20 minutes)

Pray It

◆ I Saw One of Them
(10 minutes)

Live It

◆ Organize a parish drive
◆ Work camp
◆ Souper bowl for caring
◆ Catholic organizations

Overview

Social justice is the dimension of Catholic morality that addresses such social issues as war, terrorism, world hunger, poverty, homelessness, and pollution. To participate in the global community, serve others, and work for justice, young people need to learn the Catholic teaching on social justice. This session explores Catholic social teaching—from its roots in the Trinity to its foundations in the Scriptures and natural law—as the basis for a commitment to a life of service and justice.

Outcomes

◆ The learner will recognize that God calls human society to reflect the loving relationship within the Trinity.
◆ The learner will understand the four foundations of Catholic social teaching: the common good, political responsibility, human dignity, and solidarity.
◆ The learner will discover the biblical roots of social justice.
◆ The learner will explore the interdependent relationship between service and justice.

Background Reading

◆ This session covers pages 216–225 of *The Catholic Faith Handbook for Youth*.
◆ For further exploration, check out paragraph numbers 1877–1948 of the *Catechism*.
◆ Scriptural connections: Isa. 58:6–7 (false and true worship), Amos 5:11–12 (Injustice will be repaid.), Luke 14:13–14 (Welcome the lowly.), Luke 16:19–31 (the rich man and Lazarus the beggar), Matt. 25:31–46 (the judgment of the nations)

◆ *Catholic Youth Bible* article connections: "If You Want Peace, Work for Justice" (Isa. 58:6–7), "Prayer That Does Justice" (Amos 5:21–24), "You Did It to Me" (Matt. 25:31–46)

Core Session

Catholic Social Teaching (45 minutes)

Preparation

- Gather the following items:
  - ❑ copies of handout 4, "Social Justice," one for each participant
  - ❑ copies of handout 5, "Key Concepts Underlying Catholic Social Teaching," one for each participant
  - ❑ a tape player or a CD player
  - ❑ a song with lively tempo or beat
  - ❑ newsprint
  - ❑ markers
  - ❑ masking tape
  - ❑ magazines and newspapers
  - ❑ scissors
  - ❑ glue
  - ❑ a *Catholic Youth Bible* or other Bible
- Write each of the following phrases at the top of a separate sheet of newsprint: "The Common Good," "Responsibility of the Political Authority," "Human Dignity," and "Human Solidarity."
- Review the summary points in step 7 of this session and the relevant material on pages 216–219 of the *CFH*. Be prepared to share the information with the young people.

1. Gather the participants in a circle to play a traditional game of musical chairs. Play until one person is declared the winner.

2. Next, play the game this way: each time the music stops, eliminate one chair, but keep the number of players the same. The participants must find a way for everyone to sit on a chair. Continue playing until one chair remains and all the participants are trying to figure out how to sit on that chair.

3. Debrief the activity by asking the participants the following questions:

- What was it like to play musical chairs this new way?
- What can this activity tell us about the kind of world we want to live in?

(This activity is adapted from Church World Service, "We Can Do That Too! Simulations.")

4. Post the four sheets of newsprint side by side. Distribute handout 5. Alternate the activity between the handout and the newsprint as follows:

- Invite one participant to read the paragraph on handout 5 about the common good. Referring to the sheet of newsprint titled "The Common Good," ask the participants to brainstorm what that phrase might mean in practical terms. Ask them to think of local and global issues. List them on the newsprint.
- Invite one participant to read the paragraph on handout 5 about the responsibility of the political authority. Refer to the "Responsibility of the Political Authority" newsprint, and ask the participants to give concrete examples of how the local or national government, as a political authority, takes responsibility for justice in society. List the examples on the newsprint.
- Invite one participant to read the paragraph on handout 5 about human dignity. Refer to the newsprint titled "Human Dignity," and ask the participants to brainstorm the various ways our culture deprives people of their dignity. List them on the newsprint.
- Invite one participant to read the paragraph on handout 5 about human solidarity. Refer to the "Human Solidarity" newsprint, and ask the participants to brainstorm groups of people who suffer or who deserve better treatment, but whose needs mainstream society might neglect out of ignorance, prejudice, or indifference. List the suggestions on the newsprint.

5. Divide the participants into four groups. If the groups have more than eight participants, divide them again so that the group size is six to eight members. Assign each group one of the four foundational principles of Catholic social teaching. Give the groups the corresponding sheet of newsprint, or post the newsprint close to the group that is working on the topic.

6. The task for each group is as follows:

- **The Common Good.** Using magazines and newspapers, create a collage that illustrates the common good and the ways in which people can work toward it. Find pictures that represent both the various issues about the common good that we brainstormed earlier and the foundational principles described on handout 5. Match these pictures with words or phrases

Mediaconnections

- Watch one of the following movies:
  - ◇ *With Honors* (Warner Studios, 101 minutes, 1994, rated PG-13)
  - ◇ *Dances with Wolves* (MGM Studios, 181 minutes, 1990, rated PG-13)
  - ◇ *The Fugitive* (Warner Studios, 161 minutes, 1993, rated PG-13)
  - ◇ *The Rainmaker* (Paramount Studios, 137 minutes, 1997, rated PG-13)

In each movie the main character addresses an injustice. Talk about the injustice, whom it affects, what happens, and what the results are.

- Check out these Web sites that provide information on correcting injustices in the world:
  - ◇ *www.usccb.org/cchd* (Catholic Campaign for Human Development)
  - ◇ *www.usccb.org/sdwp* (Social Development and World Peace)
  - ◇ *www.usccb.org/prolife* (Pro-Life Activities)
  - ◇ *www.childrensdefense.org* (Children's Defense Fund)
  - ◇ *www.centeronhunger.org* (Center on Hunger and Poverty)
  - ◇ *www.deathpenalty.org* (Death Penalty Focus)

JournalACTIVITIES

◆ How does your relationship with others enable you to be a reflection of the Trinity?

◆ List some of the ways that your individual moral choices affect society.

◆ Reflect on the following quote: "You have not lived a perfect day, even though you have earned your money, unless you have done something for someone who will never be able to repay you" (Ruth Smeltzer).

◆ Write a letter to God asking for strength to stand up to injustice. Wait a day or two, and then re-read your letter. How have you been strong when faced with injustice?

that illustrate ways of responding to the issues about the common good. For example, if a common-good issue is the environment, you would match a picture of a beautiful landscape with words like "clean," "reduce, reuse, recycle," "simplicity," and so forth.

- **Responsibility of the Political Authority.** Based on the issues about the responsibility of the political authority that we brainstormed earlier and the principles described on handout 5, identify several issues that are appropriate for the political authority to handle. Develop a radio ad for a politician who is ready to be committed and honest about the responsibility that the government has for these issues.
- **Human Dignity.** By reading one of two Scripture passages, John 8:3–11 or Matthew 5:23–24, investigate how Jesus promotes human dignity. Identify the important thing that Jesus says or does. Name the values that the passage reflects. Adapt the passage to show how a Christian would follow those values today. Consider how the Scripture passage connects with the brainstormed list of what is needed to respect human dignity and with the principles of human dignity described on handout 5.
- **Human Solidarity.** Using the stereotypes, prejudices, and other practices of inequality from the brainstormed list and the principles described on handout 5, create a TV commercial or a song that promotes caring for and standing with all those who need our care and support.

Each group should be prepared to show and to explain its work at the end of the allotted time. Allow about 15 minutes.

7. Draw the participants' attention to the interconnectedness of their various presentations. Conduct a presentation on social justice using key phrases from step 6 and the bullet points below, which are taken from pages 216–219 of the *CFH:*

- By our very nature, we are social beings, linked to the rest of humanity whether we like it or not.
- When we say that we are made in the image and likeness of God, it means that we reflect what God is like. But what is God like? One way to answer this question is to examine our belief in the Holy Trinity, the three persons in one God. The Trinity tells us that God isn't just a lone individual; God is a community of persons, living in perfect love and charity.
- If we are to live out our divine destiny, we must treat one another in a way that resembles the unity of the three persons in one God.
- Our love for God must translate into a love for all people and a commitment to treat them justly.
- The moral principles God calls society to follow and the moral judgments God calls society to make in order to ensure the rights of individuals and groups is called social justice.
- Social justice has deep roots in the Bible.

- Catholic social-justice teachings are based on some key concepts. By applying these concepts to different social issues, the Church makes judgments about the correct direction to follow.

   8. Invite the group to discuss their earlier presentations in the context of this wider understanding of Catholic teaching on social justice. How do these presentations reflect the life of the Trinity?

   9. To close the session, ask the following question to encourage the participants to reflect on ways they can live these Catholic social teachings: What one thing have you learned in the session that you can put into practice in the coming week?

   10. Be sure to note that the content of this session was drawn from chapter 22 of the *CFH*. Encourage the participants to read and review it in the next few days.

Session Extensions

The Social Justice Two-Step (15 minutes)

Preparation

- Gather the following items:
  - ❑ index cards of two different colors
  - ❑ markers
  - ❑ masking tape
- Review the diagram "Two Feet of Service and Justice," on page 224 of *The Catholic Faith Handbook for Youth (CFH)*.

   1. Begin the session by conducting a brief presentation on the characteristics of service work and justice work and the bullet points below, which are taken from pages 224–225 of the *CFH:*

- Both service and justice are needed as part of our response to social injustice. Works of service are more immediate, and often the results are easier to see. Works of justice are more long term, more complex to deal with, and the results may never come. But Christ calls us to be faithful—though not necessarily successful—and he will strengthen and guide us in this work.
- Charity and justice are like two feet that walk together in our faith.
- On the one hand, we must try to alleviate immediate needs by giving food to the hungry, clothing to the naked, comfort to the sick and the imprisoned, and so on. This is sometimes called the work of service, or charity.

- On the other hand, we must also work to change the structures of society that keep people hungry or poor or cause them to commit crimes. This is called the work of justice.
- Some of the social-justice issues are war, abortion, workers' rights, world hunger, and the environment.

2. Invite the participants to think about whether they prefer service work or justice work. Give an index card of one color to those whose preference is service work and an index card of the other color to those whose preference is justice work.

3. Invite the participants to write on their card what specific service or justice work they have done or would like to do. If they are unsure of the difference, point out that service work is anything that eases immediate needs by providing food, comfort, shelter, clothing, and so on, and that justice work is anything that addresses the social structures that contribute to hunger, loneliness, poverty, oppression, or homelessness—from standing up to a group of bullies to writing to a legislator about a cause to protesting. If time allows, invite those who are comfortable doing so to share the kind of work they wrote on their index cards and why. When the participants are done speaking, they can tape the cards to one of their shoes. Those who prefer service work should tape it to their right shoe; those who prefer justice work should tape it to their left shoe.

4. When everyone is through sharing, ask the participants to stand on the foot with the index card taped to it. Invite the participants to get around the world (symbolized by getting around the room) on only one foot. (If you have any participants who cannot stand, have them tape the card to one side of whatever their mode of conveyance is. They are restricted to moving to that side when the rest of the group is hopping.) After the participants have hopped around for a minute, stop them. Then ask, Is this the way you want to encounter the world?

5. Ask the participants to find a partner who prefers the other kind of work (or ask them to find someone with an index card of a different color). Invite the participants to take turns hopping this time, holding on to each other for balance. Ask if this is an easier way to get around in the world. Then ask if it is as easy as walking on two feet.

6. Ask those who prefer service work to think of one work of justice they can do that is related to the service work they enjoy and to write it on a new card of the justice color. Ask those who prefer justice work to think of one work of service they could do that is related to the justice work they

enjoy and to write it on a new card of the service color. The participants then tape justice-colored cards to the left shoe and service-colored cards to the right shoe. Invite the participants to get around the world again on the feet that have cards taped to them. They should be walking on both feet. Ask them again to share whether this is an easier way to get around.

7. Invite the participants to make a commitment to do one act of service and one act of justice in the near future. If they need suggestions for justice action steps, mention examples such as writing a letter to the editor of the newspaper or to a legislator, participating in a prayer event at an abortion clinic, or engaging in some kind of boycott or protest. If they need suggestions for causes, use the index cards from step 3.

We Lift It Up to You, Lord (20 minutes)

Preparation

- Gather the following items:
  - ❏ newspaper news sections that feature current issues
  - ❏ masking tape
  - ❏ markers, one for each small group
  - ❏ paper, one sheet for each small group
  - ❏ pens or pencils, one for each small group
- Create one large newspaper panel by laying pages of newspaper side by side to form a square large enough for the group to stand around. Be sure that the sheets you are using contain plenty of news articles. Tape the square together with masking tape on the underside of the newspaper.

1. In pairs or in small groups of three, invite the participants to read the articles nearest them and to select one that addresses a social justice issue. With a marker, they should circle the article. Ask each group to name out loud and in brief terms the issue that the article discusses.

2. Provide each group with a blank sheet of paper and a pencil or a pen. Ask each group to compose a brief prayer of intercession based on its selected article. Allow a few minutes for discussion and writing.

3. Invite the participants to sit around the newspaper square close to the article their group selected. Explain that one person from each group, by means of a prayer of intercession, will "lift up," or "make holy," that section of the newspaper square. As each prayer is offered, the small group will hold up its part of the newspaper. Invite the participants to respond to each prayer by saying, "Help us to do your work, Lord." By the time the whole group has finished, the participants should be holding the large newspaper panel at shoulder level or higher.

4. Conclude with the following comment:

- Many times we see a situation from only one viewpoint instead of from a broad perspective. God sees the situation holistically. We have raised up to God the concerns that we see in our world today. We pray that we remember to see with God's eyes and continue to respond to the needs of others. Amen.

I Saw One of Them (10 minutes)

Preparation

- Gather the following items:
  - ❑ copies of handout 6, "I Saw One of Them," one for each participant
  - ❑ a *Catholic Youth Bible* or other Bible
  - ❑ a tape player or a CD player
  - ❑ a song with the theme of justice, such as "The Summons," by John L. Bell
- Recruit a reader to proclaim Matthew 25:31–40.

Introduce the prayer with the following or similar words:

- Today we come together to learn how our faith calls us to serve others. In our prayer we recall Jesus' words about feeding the hungry and clothing the naked. We'll reflect on those words through a poem by Lawrence Ferlinghetti. When we come to the reflection part of the poem, each of us will read a line of it. Starting with the person on my left, each one in turn will read a line, beginning with "I saw . . ."

Continue with the prayer as outlined on handout 6.

Options and Actions

- **Organize a parish drive.** Invite young people to contact a local soup kitchen, shelter, senior center, or other social-service agency to ask what kinds of items it needs. A senior center may need warm socks and gloves

Spirit & Song
Connections

- ◆ "The Summons," by John L. Bell
- ◆ "What Is Our Service to Be," by Scot Crandal
- ◆ "Ven al Banquete / Come to the Feast," by Bob Hurd

for its clients. A shelter may need small, travel-size toiletry items (tooth-brush, toothpaste, shampoo, soap). A soup kitchen may need certain canned foods. Organize a parishwide collection of the items.

- **Work camp.** Research and participate in some work camp or justice immersion programs. Experience firsthand the difference you can make in the life of others by repairing homes, building schools, teaching children, working with homeless people, and so forth. Check out Young Neighbors in Action, a service learning experience for high school youth, sponsored by the Center for Ministry Development (CMD). Information about the program is on the CMD Web site, *www.cmdnet.org.*
- **Souper Bowl of Caring.** Check out this annual fundraiser for local charities, held each year on Super Bowl Sunday. Get your parish involved in donating money to a local charity of your choice. To see how this event works, check out the Web site *www.souperbowl.org* or call 800-358-SOUP (7687) for more information and resources.
- **Catholic organizations.** The article "Catholic Service Organizations for Charity and Justice," on page 218 in *The Catholic Faith Handbook for Youth,* describes three of the largest such organizations. Invite young people to explore the Web sites listed, or order brochures to share with them. Explore whether you can do anything as a group for one of these organizations.

Familyconnections

- ◆ Organize a discussion group for parents that focuses on helping them connect with their young person on justice issues. Possible topics include dealing with ethical issues in the workplace, making conscious family choices to live simply, and shopping with conscience.
- ◆ Volunteer as a family at a local soup kitchen.
- ◆ Participate in the program Adopt-a-Family-for-Christmas through a local social-service agency such as Catholic Charities.
- ◆ During the Lenten season, participate with your family in Operation Rice Bowl, sponsored by Catholic Relief Services (*www.catholicrelief.org*).

Social Justice

This session covers pages 216–225 of *The Catholic Faith Handbook for Youth*. For further exploration, check out paragraph numbers 1877–1948 of the *Catechism of the Catholic Church*.

Session Summary

- By our very nature, we are social beings, linked to the rest of humanity whether we like it or not.
- When we say that we are made in the image and likeness of God, it means that we reflect what God is like. But what is God like? One way to answer this question is to examine our belief in the Holy Trinity, the three persons in one God. The Trinity tells us that God isn't just a lone individual; God is a community of persons, living in perfect love and charity.
- If we are to live out our divine destiny, we must treat one another in a way that resembles the unity of the three persons in one God.
- Our love for God must translate into a love for all people and a commitment to treat them justly.
- The moral principles God calls society to follow and the moral judgments God calls society to make in order to ensure the rights of individuals and groups is called social justice.
- Social justice has deep roots in the Bible. For example, Isaiah 58:6–7, NRSV (false and true worship), Amos 5:11–12, NRSV (Injustice will be repaid.), Luke 14:13–14, NRSV (welcoming the lowly), Luke 16:19–31, NRSV (the rich man and Lazarus the beggar), Matthew 25:31–46, NRSV (the judgment of the nations).
- Catholic social-justice teachings are based on some key concepts. By applying these concepts to different social issues, the Church makes judgments about the correct direction to follow.
- Both service and justice are needed as part of our response to social injustice. Works of service are more immediate, and often the results are easier to see. Works of justice are more long term, more complex to deal with, and the results may never come. But Christ calls us to be faithful—though not necessarily successful—and he will strengthen and guide us in this work.
- Charity and justice are like two feet that walk together in our faith.
- On the one hand, we must try to alleviate immediate needs by giving food to the hungry, clothing to the naked, comfort to the sick and the imprisoned, and so on. This is sometimes called the work of service, or charity.

- On the other hand, we must also work to change the structures of society that keep people hungry or poor or cause them to commit crimes. This is called the work of justice.
- Some of the social-justice issues are war, abortion, workers' rights, world hunger, and the environment.

    (All summary points are taken from *The Catholic Faith Handbook for Youth,* by Brian Singer-Towns et al. [Winona, MN: Saint Mary's Press, 2004], pages 216–225. Copyright © 2004 by Saint Mary's Press. All rights reserved.)

Talk Points

- What ideas do you have for structuring society so that it would be easier for those who are poor to obtain what they need for a full life?
- Pay attention to stories of injustice in the news, and, as a family, choose a topic of concern. Brainstorm a list of acts of service and a list of acts of justice to respond to that concern, and then choose one item from each list that you can engage in as a family. (This activity is adapted from Karen Emmerich, *Justice: Building God's Reign* [Winona, MN: Saint Mary's Press, 1997], page 37. Copyright © 1997 by Saint Mary's Press. All rights reserved.)
- Discuss the ways in which the values of Catholic social teaching are best exemplified in the world, locally and globally. How does your family reflect those values?

Key Concepts Underlying Catholic Social Teaching

Catholic social-justice teachings are based on some key concepts. By applying these concepts to different social issues, the Church makes judgments about the correct direction to follow. In this session we will look briefly at the following four key concepts, which are taken from pages 219–223 of *The Catholic Faith Handbook for Youth.*

1. The Common Good. When conditions exist in society that allow all people, either as groups or individuals, to reach their human and spiritual fulfillment more fully and more easily, the common good is achieved. It is important that we understand what the common good really means; it isn't just doing the greatest good for the greatest number of people. The decision's impact on each and every person must be taken into account.

2. Responsibility of the Political Authority. Although some people may be cynical about politics and government, the Church teaches that political authority (also called the state) has an important role: to defend and promote the common good of civil society. Policy makers at all levels of government should ensure that each person has access to the resources needed to lead a truly human life: "food, clothing, health, work, education and culture, suitable information, the right to establish a family, and so on"[1] (*CCC,* number 1908). These needs are often referred to as basic human rights.

3. Human Dignity. The homeless man on the street, the immigrant who crosses our borders illegally, even the prisoners in our jails all share the same human dignity that we have (remember Matthew 25:31–46, NRSV). Because of this God calls us to consider each and every human being as "another self" (*CCC,* number 1944).

4. Human Solidarity. Solidarity means that we are to think in terms of friendship and charity toward our brothers and sisters in society. We are one. It's like being connected by invisible threads to every other person in the world. When one of us is suffering, that suffering is transferred down that invisible thread to all of us. As a starting point, solidarity means distributing the world's resources so that each of us gets our fair share and no one is suffering because of physical need.

1. Cf. *Gaudium et spes* 26 § 2.

I Saw One of Them

Leader: Let us take a moment to collect ourselves and to know that we are in the presence of God. *(Pause.)*

In the name of the Father and of the Son and of the Holy Spirit.

All: Amen.

All: I call upon you, for you will answer me, O God;
   incline your ear to me, hear my words.

. . . .

   Guard me as the apple of the eye;
   hide me in the shadow of your wings.

(Psalm 17:6,8, NRSV)

Reading. Matthew 25:31–40, NRSV

Song.

Reflection.

#89

I saw one of them sleeping huddled under cardboard by the Church
   of Saint Francis
I saw one of them rousted by the priest
I saw one of them squatting in bushes
I saw another staggering against the plate glass window of a first-class
   restaurant
I saw one of them in a phone booth shaking it
I saw one with burlap feet
I saw one in a grocery store come out with a pint
I saw another come out with nothing
I saw another putting a rope through the loops of his pants
I saw one with a bird on his shoulder
I saw one of them singing on the steps of City Hall in the so cool city of
   love
I saw one of them trying to give a lady cop a hug
I saw another sleeping by the Brooklyn Bridge
I saw another standing by the Golden Gate
The view from there was great

All: God, you call us to your service and to continue your saving work among us. May your love never abandon us. Amen!

(The poem in this handout is "#89," in *A Far Rockaway of the Heart,* by Lawrence Ferlinghetti [New York: New Directions, 1997], page 107. Copyright © 1997 by Lawrence Ferlinghetti. Used with permission of New Directions Publishing.)

Overview

God reveals moral truths to us in various ways. First, God places in each of us the natural law, that is, the human nature to know right and wrong. God, through the Church, also provides us with the Scriptures and the Tradition of the Church as tools for discerning the moral truth. Young people today are living in a time when society often presents moral choices as purely subjective. It is important for youth to learn that God and the Church have provided concrete sources for discerning answers to moral questions. This session explores the fact that all moral truth comes from God, and it also suggest ways for young people to integrate the laws from God and the Church with the formation of their conscience.

Outcomes

◆ The learner will recognize natural law as part of human nature.

◆ The learner will appreciate the relationship between the Old Law (the Ten Commandments) and the New Law (the law of the Gospel).

◆ The learner will be able to identify the laws, or precepts, of the Church.

◆ The learner will discover ways to integrate these laws with the formation of conscience.

Background Reading

◆ This session covers pages 226–235 of *The Catholic Faith Handbook for Youth*.

◆ For further exploration, check out paragraph numbers 1776–1802, 1949–1986, and 2030–2051 of the *Catechism*.

◆ Scriptural connections: Exod. 20:1–17 (the Ten Commandments), Matt. 5:1—6:34 (the Sermon on the Mount)

◆ *Catholic Youth Bible* article connections: "The Ten Commandments" (Exod. 20:1–17), "A Lord's Prayer Reflection" (Matt. 6:5–15)

Core Session

Teach the Children (45 minutes)

Preparation

- Gather the following items:
  - ❑ copies of handout 7, "Sources of Moral Truth," one for each participant
  - ❑ newsprint
  - ❑ markers
- Review the summary points in step 3 of this session and the relevant material on pages 226–235 of *The Catholic Faith Handbook for Youth (CFH)*. Be prepared to share the information with the young people.

   1. As a large group, brainstorm the types of moral dilemmas that youth between the ages of nine and twelve face daily. If some participants have younger brothers or sisters, they will have firsthand knowledge of such situations. Others might remember what it was like to be those ages. List the situations or issues on newsprint. If the group struggles to come up with ideas, be prepared to toss in your thoughts to promote the discussion, including examples such as disobeying parents and cheating in school.

   2. Divide the participants into small groups of three or four. Ask each group to select the moral dilemma faced by young people that they would choose to portray or role-play for a group of younger children. Be sure that each small group selects a different scenario.

   3. Conduct a presentation on the sources of moral truth, using key phrases from step 1 and the bullet points below, which are taken from pages 226–235 of the *CFH*.

- Each of us has a natural ability to tell right from wrong. Some people rely on this natural ability when making most of their moral choices. But because of outside influences, this natural ability can often be mistaken or in error, which is why God has also provided us with "instruction manuals," found in the Scriptures and Tradition.

Mediaconnections

◆ Watch a movie with a "Golden Rule" theme, such as *It's a Wonderful Life* (Republic Studios, 132 minutes, 1947, NR, suitable for all); *It Could Happen to You* (Columbia/TriStar, 101 minutes, 1994, rated PG); or *Willow* (Metro-Goldwyn-Mayer, 126 minutes, 1988, rated PG). How do the main characters try to live by the Golden Rule? What makes it difficult for them? What are the rewards for living such a life?

◆ Review music video clips, magazines, or song lyrics, and compare and contrast the media's portrayal of love with Jesus' teaching about love.

◆ Arrange a visit to a local media company (radio or television station, newspaper, or advertising agency). Invite the participants to prepare ahead of time some questions related to how the media affect our decision making and overall morality.

- It is important for us to know these laws and teachings—particularly as they are taught by the Magisterium (the pope and bishops)—in order to live the moral life God intends for us to live.
- The moral law that we are born with is called natural law because it is part of our human nature. Saint Thomas Aquinas describes natural law as "nothing other than the light of understanding placed in us by God; through it we know what we must do and what we must avoid"[1] (*CCC*, no. 1955). Because we are made in God's image, the natural moral law enables us to participate in God's wisdom and goodness.
- However, it is obvious from much of the evil in the world that not everyone perceives clearly and immediately the positive dictates of natural law. So God provides other ways of revealing moral truth to us.
- The Law of Moses, also called the Old Law, was the first stage of God's Revelation to us about how we are to live as people made in God's image. This Old Law is summarized in the Ten Commandments that God revealed to Moses on Mount Sinai (Exod. 20:1–17).
- The Ten Commandments are a special expression of natural law, making perfectly clear through God's Revelation what he had already placed in the human heart.
- The Old Law is the first stage on the way to the Kingdom of God, preparing us for conversion and faith in Jesus. In this way the Old Law is a preparation for the Gospel.
- The New Law, or the Law of the Gospel, is the perfection of God's moral law, both natural and revealed. Jesus modeled the New Law, and taught the core of it in his Sermon on the Mount, when he gave us the Beatitudes to teach us what we must be like to inherit the Kingdom of God.
- Jesus' New Law does not abolish or devalue the Ten Commandments, but instead releases their full potential.
- As members of the Church, the Body of Christ, we are called to live a moral life. Christ has given the Church the responsibility of being a light to the world and a model of his New Law of love. The Church does this through its moral teaching. In addition, the Church has laws for its members that help guide us toward the moral life, the good actions and attitudes that are our ongoing spiritual worship.
- Previous chapters have already presented how God has given the Magisterium, that is, the bishops of the world united with the Pope, the responsibility for passing on and teaching the Tradition. Tradition includes the moral teaching of Christ's New Law, and so the Magisterium is always applying Christ's moral teaching to modern situations.
- Many voices in the world today try to tell you what is right and what is wrong. Many of them are giving you advice that is contrary to the Law of Christ. That is why in forming your conscience it is essential that you stay connected to your Church and the opportunities it provides for dialogue,

reading, and reflection. The Scriptures and Tradition can light the path in our conscience formation, but only if we absorb it in faith and prayer, and put it into practice. Acting on things that you know are good is the kind of practice that will keep your conscience in shape.

4. Provide the small groups with the following instructions:
- Using the sources of moral truth present in the Ten Commandments and the Beatitudes, address the situation assigned to your group, and develop a short one-act play to present to a group of young children.
- Remember that people younger than you might not understand the nuances of moral decision making as you do, so you will need to use actions and words that they can understand.
- You can use the Bible. You can find more information on the Old Law of the Ten Commandments and on the New Law of Jesus on pages 228–230 of the *CFH*.
- Focus on writing the dialogue for the various players.
- Include an introduction and a conclusion in your presentation. Walking in and doing a short play without these two elements will diminish the play's effectiveness.
- The conclusion needs to have the "moral" of the skit presented in a clear and easily understood statement, such as, "Don't judge a book by its cover."

5. If time permits, invite a few or all of the small groups to present their role-plays. Invite the participants to respond to the following questions:
- What was it like trying to use the elements of moral law to illustrate how to make a decision?
- What did you learn from this experience?
- What do you think children could learn from your play?
- How do you think the children, after viewing your play, will approach the moral law in the future?

Conclude by noting that the content of this session was drawn from chapter 23 of the *CFH*. Encourage the participants to read and review it in the next few days.

Session Extensions

Church Law Rooted in Old Law and New Law (20 minutes)

Preparation
- Gather the following items:
  - ❑ copies of handout 8, "The Precepts of the Church," one for each participant

TryThis

In collaboration with the parish director of religious education or a Catholic school principal or teacher, set up a time for your entire group to perform their plays for an audience of young children. If time allows, have members of your group conduct a brief question-and-answer session with the children after the presentation. Later, debrief the experience with the participants.

Familyconnections

◆ Talk about how your family is a "Beatitude family." How are the Beatitudes lived out each day in your family?

◆ Write up family commandments based on the Ten Commandments. Post them on the refrigerator or bulletin board where family members will see them every day.

◆ Suggest that the participants talk with their parents or guardians about how the latter follow their conscience when making moral decisions. Ask them what Scripture passages have been helpful to them and whom they have consulted to learn about the Church's teaching on a particular subject.

◆ Suggest that the participants encourage their families to choose a moral issue that is a special concern. Family members can prepare a Catholic response after researching the applicable Scripture teaching and the Church's teaching.

❑ newsprint
❑ markers
❑ pens or pencils
❑ copies of *The Catholic Faith Handbook for Youth (CFH),* one for each participant
❑ a *Catholic Youth Bible* or other Bible

• Review the seven precepts of the Church on pages 230–231 of the *CFH*.
• Number the newsprint with numbers 1 through 7 along the left side. Next to each number, print a large "O" and a large "N," with enough space in between them to record a check mark.

1. Begin by distributing a pen or pencil and a copy of handout 8 to each participant. Tell the participants that they may work alone or in groups of their own choosing.

2. Provide the participants with the following instructions:
• You are on a quest to uncover the roots of the seven examples of Church law on the handout. You might be able to uncover only one or two roots, or you might discover several. Try to discover the roots of all seven examples, and write down as many as you come up with.
• You might find in the Old Testament some roots of the Old Law of the Ten Commandments. You might discover in the New Testament some roots of the New Law of Jesus Christ. Some Church precepts might have roots in both the Old Testament and the New Testament; others might have roots in just one of them.
• You can use the *CFH* and the Bible in your search.
• If you find a root in the Old Law, write on the handout either the place in the Old Testament where you found it or which commandment you think it is.
• If you find a root in the New Law, write on the handout a few words to describe the New Testament story that it comes from, or you can write the chapter and verse number of the New Testament passage that contains the root.

3. While the participants are working, you can give them hints, for example, the location of the Ten Commandments in the Scriptures (Exod. 20:1–17 or Deut. 5:1–21), where the Beatitudes are listed (Matt. 5:1—6:34), a suggestion about the loaves and the fishes, the Last Supper, the Emmaus story in relation to the Eucharist, and so on.

4. When everyone is done, record the results, 1 through 7, by placing a check mark next to the large "O" when anyone suggests a root in the Old Law and next to the large "N" when anyone suggests a root in the New Law for that particular Church law. Invite someone advocating a particular root to explain why the Church law stems from a certain Old or New Law. Invite others to add reasons if the first person didn't name all of them. Gently challenge any reasons or connections that seem too far off the mark.

5. Close the session by suggesting to the participants that when they hear about a Church precept, they might want to investigate where the precept has its roots: in the natural law, in the Old Law of the Ten Commandments, or in the New Law of Jesus Christ revealed in the New Testament. Explain this statement too: "The Ten Commandments are a special expression of natural law, making perfectly clear through God's Revelation what he had already placed in the human heart"(*CFH,* pp. 228–229).

What If . . . ? (15 minutes)

1. Invite the participants to select a partner. Direct all the pairs to stand up and form two circles, one inside the other, with one partner in the inner circle and one partner in the outer circle. Ask the partners to face each other.

2. Announce that you will read a number of "What if . . . ?" questions, each describing a situation that the participants may or may not have experienced. After each question, all the participants will share with their partners their response to the questions and the reasoning for their answer. After 45 to 60 seconds, ask the outer circle to rotate one person to the right. Then read another "What if . . . ?" question. Repeat this process, with a new question for each round, until time is up. Stress the importance of providing not only the answer but also the moral reasoning that led to it.

3. Use the following "What if . . . ?" questions, or create your own:

- What if a friend has asked you to read her English paper, but it is not very good. You know that she will not get a good grade unless she makes some changes. What do you say to her?
- What if you are buying some new clothes at the mall, and the clerk gives you ten dollars too much in change? What if the clerk gives you only one dollar too much?
- What if you are with a group of friends, and they begin to put down someone you know?
- What if a friend confides in you about being involved in some vandalism at your school? You later hear that the police have accused another person who you know was not involved. How do you respond?
- What if you've found the perfect part-time job as an office assistant, with great pay? One day your boss gives you some papers to shred. The papers show that the company has been releasing poisonous chemicals into the local river. What do you do?

TryThis

For participants who are ready for an extra challenge, get a copy of a recent pastoral statement from the United States Conference of Catholic Bishops. Invite the participants to seek out the roots of the statement in the Old Law and in the New Law.

JournalACTIVITIES

- How can you present the moral viewpoint of Jesus and of the Church enthusiastically and without apology?
- Write a story about a time when you did something contrary to your conscience. What happened? How did you feel? What did you do about it?
- Select a Beatitude at the beginning of each day, and keep it in mind throughout the day. At the end of the day, answer these questions: How did I see this Beatitude come to life today? What does this Beatitude mean for me?
- Which commandment do you find the most difficult to live out?

TryThis

Instead of using the list of "What if . . . ?" questions, ask the participants to brainstorm their own list of questions. They can write down various scenarios and turn them in anonymously.

TryThis

Using the article "Doing the Right Thing" (*CFH,* p. 207), invite a few participants to role-play the situation described in the article. Then lead a discussion to determine what the right decision is. Invite the participants to share not only what the right decision is but also the reasoning that leads to the decision.

4. To wrap up this activity, have a discussion with the participants about the ease or the difficulty they had with this activity.

(This activity is adapted from Brian Singer-Towns, *Deciding as a Christian,* p. 22.)

Forming Your Conscience (15 minutes)

Preparation
- Gather the following items:
  - ❏ copies of *The Catholic Faith Handbook for Youth (CFH),* one for each participant
  - ❏ sheets of blank paper, one for each participant
  - ❏ newsprint
  - ❏ pens or pencils
- Familiarize yourself with the article "Top Ten Ways for Forming Your Conscience," on page 234 of the *CFH.*

1. Invite the participants to read the article "Top Ten Ways for Forming Your Conscience," on page 234 of the *CFH.* In place of each of these ten ways for forming the conscience, ask them to say the same thing and to write their "translation" in a list format on the left side of their paper.

2. Ask for volunteers to share their translation of the ways to form the conscience.

3. Next, direct the participants to assign a number between 1 and 10 (1 = never; 10 = frequently) to each way of forming the conscience, corresponding with how often they take advantage of each method. They can assign the same numerical value to different methods. Let them know that their paper is confidential and will not be shared with the group.

4. As a follow-up to assigning the rating numbers, ask them to write down one way in which they make better use of each method of forming their conscience. Encourage them to be creative. For example, instead of just writing "go to Mass more" for the first method, write "go to 9:30 Mass with my family and try to pay attention during the entire Mass."

5. Lead the participants in sharing the suggestions they have come up with. Keep a list of the suggestions on newsprint.

6. As a group, commit to one of the suggestions everyone can do each time you gather. Follow up on this commitment every time you meet.

Examining Our Choices (10 minutes)

Preparation

- Gather the following items:
  - ❑ sheets of blank paper, several for each small group
  - ❑ pens or pencils

   1. Divide the participants into four groups. Assign each group one of the following themes:
- relationship with God
- relationship with family
- relationship with the wider community
- relationship with friends

Invite each small group to write two prayers of intercession for its assigned theme.

   2. Begin with the sign of the cross, and then offer the following words:
- We enter into prayer today by offering to God our thoughts, hopes, needs, and concerns. We bring to God prayers of intercession for ourself and for others. I invite two people from each group to stand and read the two prayers your group has written. After each prayer, respond, "To you we turn, O God."

   3. Next ask the participants to close their eyes and reflect on the following questions. Allow at least 20 to 30 seconds for reflection following each question.
- Have I taken full advantage of the gifts of the Eucharist and the Mass?
- Have I taken time to examine my conscience and the decisions I have made?
- Have I taken advantage of the sacrament of Reconciliation to repair and restore my broken relationships?
- Have I spent time with the sacred Scriptures to reflect on their application to my daily life?
- Have I devoted ample time for prayer, not just to ask for things but to listen for the response in my heart?
- Have I taken the teachings of the Church to heart when faced with daily decisions?
- Do I see every choice I make as an opportunity to grow closer to God?
- Am I sensitive to what I allow to enter my mind through movies, television, music, games, and computers?

Spirit & Song connections

- ◆ "I Will Lift My Eyes," by Cyprian Consiglio
- ◆ "Open My Eyes," by Jesse Manibusan
- ◆ "Revive Us, O God," by Jesse Manibusan

- Do I have role models who set a high standard for me to achieve in leading a virtuous life?
- Do I seek out the truth and not readily accept what popular opinion or gossip says?

4. Conclude the prayer time by praying together the Act of Hope or the Act of Love, from *The Catholic Faith Handbook for Youth,* p. 381.

Options and Actions

- **Understanding conscience.** On newsprint draw a line down the center of the paper. On the left, list the laws that the participants brainstorm as laws that they learned about in this session. On the right, list the secular laws that they are aware of, whether in their school, town, state, or country. Then pose the following questions: How are the two lists alike? How are they different? Which type of law do you listen to most? Which source do you trust the most and why? Does the fact that a law was made by humans make it different than a law made by God?
- **Recipes of love.** A recipe is like a set of laws; it contains the things that have to be done to get a certain result. Distribute an index card or, better yet, an actual recipe card to each participant. Invite everyone to create a recipe by listing the ingredients needed to live a life of love and the instructions for making the ingredients come together well. Consider posting the "recipes" on the church's bulletin board, adding them to your parish Web site, or using them to create a recipe book.
- **Media watch.** After polling the participants about their favorite television shows, tape several of these shows. Watch the episodes as a group, stopping the tape at any point when a moral decision has to be made. Ask how the moral decision that the character made could have been reached more easily if the person had checked in with the Scriptures and Tradition.

Sources of Moral Truth

This session covers pages 226–235 of *The Catholic Faith Handbook for Youth*. For further exploration, review paragraph numbers 1776–1802, 1949–1986, and 2030–2051 of the *Catechism of the Catholic Church*.

Session Summary

- Each of us has a natural ability to tell right from wrong. Some people rely on this natural ability when making most of their moral choices. But because of outside influences, this natural ability can often be mistaken or in error, which is why God has also provided us with "instruction manuals," found in the Scriptures and Tradition.

- It is important for us to know these laws and teachings—particularly as they are taught by the Magisterium (the pope and bishops)—in order to live the moral life God intends for us to live.

- The moral law that we are born with is called natural law, because it is part of our human nature. Saint Thomas Aquinas describes natural law as "nothing other than the light of understanding placed in us by God; through it we know what we must do and what we must avoid"[1] (*CCC*, number 1955). Because we are made in God's image, the natural moral law enables us to participate in God's wisdom and goodness.

- However, it is obvious from much of the evil in the world that not everyone perceives clearly and immediately the positive dictates of natural law. So God provides other ways of revealing moral truth to us.

- The Law of Moses, also called the Old Law, was the first stage of God's Revelation to us about how we are to live as people made in God's image. This Old Law is summarized in the Ten Commandments that God revealed to Moses on Mount Sinai (Exodus 20:1–17, NRSV).

- The Ten Commandments are a special expression of natural law, making perfectly clear through God's Revelation what he had already placed in the human heart.

- The Old Law is the first stage on the way to the Kingdom of God, preparing us for conversion and faith in Jesus. In this way the Old Law is a preparation for the Gospel.

- The New Law, or the Law of the Gospel, is the perfection of God's moral law, both natural and revealed. Jesus modeled the New Law, and taught the core of it in his Sermon on the Mount, when he gave us the Beatitudes to teach us what we must be like to inherit the Kingdom of God.

- Jesus' New Law does not abolish or devalue the Ten Commandments, but instead releases their full potential.
- As members of the Church, the Body of Christ, we are called to live a moral life. Christ has given the Church the responsibility of being a light to the world and a model of his New Law of love. The Church does this through its moral teaching. In addition, the Church has laws for its members that help guide us toward the moral life, the good actions and attitudes that are our ongoing spiritual worship.
- Previous chapters have already presented how God has given the Magisterium, that is, the bishops of the world united with the Pope, the responsibility for passing on and teaching the Tradition. Tradition includes the moral teaching of Christ's New Law, and so the Magisterium is always applying Christ's moral teaching to modern situations.
- Many voices in the world today try to tell you what is right and what is wrong. Many of them are giving you advice that is contrary to the Law of Christ. That is why in forming your conscience it is essential that you stay connected to your Church and the opportunities it provides for dialogue, reading, and reflection. The Scriptures and Tradition can light the path in our conscience formation, but only if we absorb it in faith and prayer, and put it into practice. Acting on things that you know are good is the kind of practice that will keep your conscience in shape.

1. St. Thomas Aquinas, *Dec. præc.* I.

Talk Points

- To whom do you turn when you have to make a tough decision? How does this person help you? What makes you turn to this person?
- Which step of the decision-making process is hardest for you? Why?
- Share a time when you did something that went against your conscience. What happened? How did you feel? What did you do about it?
- By making a public declaration about how we choose to live out the vision and values of Jesus, we strengthen our resolve to live a moral life. Create a written declaration by listing behaviors and attitudes you will practice in living morally.

The Precepts of the Church

The precepts of the Church direct us to participate in the sacramental life of the Church so that we might be nourished for living a moral life. Following are the precepts of the Church as designated by the Catholic bishops of the United States of America (*The Catholic Faith for Youth,* pages 230–231):

1. To keep holy the day of the Lord's Resurrection; to worship God by participating in Mass every Sunday and on the holy days of obligation; to avoid those activities that would hinder renewal of the soul and body on the Sabbath (for example, needless work or unnecessary shopping).

   Can you find roots for this precept in:

   the Old Law?

   the New Law?

2. To lead a sacramental life; to receive Holy Communion frequently and the sacrament of Reconciliation regularly—minimally, to receive the sacrament of Reconciliation at least once a year (annual confession is obligatory only if serious sin is involved); minimally also, to receive Holy Communion at least once a year between the first Sunday of Lent and Trinity Sunday.

   Can you find roots for this precept in:

   the Old Law?

   the New Law?

3. To study Catholic teaching in preparation for the sacrament of Confirmation, to be confirmed, and then to continue to study and advance the cause of Christ.

   Can you find roots for this precept in:

   the Old Law?

   the New Law?

4. To observe the marriage laws of the Church; to give religious training, by example and word, to one's children; to use parish schools and catechetical programs.

   Can you find roots for this precept in:

   the Old Law?

   the New Law?

5. To strengthen and support the Church—one's own parish community and parish priests, the worldwide Church, and the Pope.

Can you find roots for this precept in:

the Old Law?

the New Law?

6. To do penance, including abstaining from meat and fasting from food on the appointed days.

Can you find roots for this precept in:

the Old Law?

the New Law?

7. To join in the missionary spirit and apostolate (work) of the Church.

Can you find roots for this precept in:

the Old Law?

the New Law?

4 Honoring God

AT A GLANCE

Study It

Core Session
◆ Putting God First
(45 minutes)

Session Extensions
◆ The Power of Proclaiming
a Name
(20 minutes)
◆ Morality Play
(20 minutes)

Pray It

◆ God Comes First
(10 minutes)

Live It

◆ God's presence
◆ Cinquain *(sin-kane)*
◆ Symbols of faith
◆ Bookmarks

Overview

Young people are hearing a wide array of voices telling them what is important for their life. They urgently need to realize that God's voice, God's relationship, is the most important one in their life. This session covers the first three of the Ten Commandments, those that concern our relationship with God, and explores how young people can put God above all things in their life, in their speech, and in their observance of the Sabbath.

Outcomes

◆ The learner will explore what it means to put God above all things.
◆ The learner will realize that everyday speech is a powerful tool for serving God.
◆ The learner will develop strategies for observing the Sabbath.

Background Reading

◆ This session covers pages 236–244 of *The Catholic Faith Handbook for Youth.*
◆ For further exploration, check out paragraph numbers 2052–2195 of the *Catechism.*
◆ Scriptural connections: Gen. 2:1–3 (creation of the Sabbath), Exod. 20:1–17 (the Ten Commandments), Matt. 7:7–8 (Ask, and you will receive.), Rom. 8:28 (Our hope is with God.)
◆ *Catholic Youth Bible* article connections: "The Sabbath" (Gen. 2:1–3), "Offering Your Day to God" (Prov. 16:3), "The Miniature Gospel" (Matt. 22:34–40), "Where Is God?" (2 Pet. 3:9)

JournalACTIVITIES

◆ For the coming week, how can you make God more of a priority in your life? What might have to change in your life for this to happen?

◆ Name the ways you love God with all your heart, all your soul, your entire mind, and all your strength.

◆ What do you believe about God? Reflect on this quote:

> If the thought comes to you that everything that you have thought about God is mistaken and that there is no God, do not be dismayed. It happens to many people. But do not think that the source of your unbelief is that there is no God. If you no longer believe in the God in whom you believed before, you must strive to grasp better that which you call God. When a savage ceases to believe in his wooden God, this does not mean that there is no God, but only that the true God is not [made] of wood.
>
> (Leo Tolstoy, as quoted by Hans Küng, *That the World May Believe,* p. 143.)

Core Session

Putting God First (45 minutes)

Preparation

• Gather the following items:
  ❏ copies of handout 9, "Honoring God," one for each participant
  ❏ sheets of paper
  ❏ pens or pencils
  ❏ newsprint
  ❏ markers

• Review the summary points in step 6 of this session and the relevant material on pages 236–244 of *The Catholic Faith Handbook for Youth (CFH).* Be prepared to share the information with the young people.

1. Distribute a sheet of paper and a pen or pencil to all participants. Ask them to think about a typical day. Have them lay out their schedule, detailing what they do at any given time during the day. Tell them to start when they wake up and to conclude when they go to bed at night.

2. After a few minutes, ask one or two participants to share a bit of their schedule with the large group. Then ask each participant to add up the amount of time spent doing different activities (watching television, eating, sleeping, going to school, and so forth). Based on their typical schedule and the amount of time spent doing certain activities, ask them to list their top five priorities. Then ask the participants to turn to the person next to them and share their responses to the following questions:

• Are you surprised by the results?
• Why or why not?
• Does your priority list reflect what is most important to you? Why or why not?

(Steps 1 and 2 are adapted from Rick Bundschuh and Tom Finley, *High School Talksheets: Psalms and Proverbs—Updated!* p. 46.)

3. Ask for a volunteer to read aloud the first three commandments, found in Exod. 20:2–11. Ask the group to brainstorm what the term *other gods* in verse 3 means. Ask them what they think the term meant for the Israelites. Then ask the participants to discuss what the term *other gods* means for us today. Point out to the participants that in addition to people, "other gods" could include things such as popularity, career, or money. List the responses on the right side of the newsprint.

4. Ask the participants to compare and contrast any similarities between the two lists. (Be sure to let the young people know that the items they come up with aren't necessarily bad, like being busy, for instance. The problem arises when being busy comes before what's truly important: putting God first.)

5. Divide the participants into small groups of four to six. Depending on the number of items on the right side of the newsprint, distribute the items evenly among the participants so that each small group has at least one item to discuss. Invite each small group to consider its list of "other gods" and to discuss these questions:

- How can these items or situations get in the way of our loving God at all times?
- What can we do to make sure these items don't become false gods in our life?

Then invite each small group to shares its insights with the large group.

6. Instruct the participants to refer to their individual priority lists. Ask by a show of hands how many of them listed God as one of their priorities. Conduct a presentation on honoring God, using key phrases from the preceding steps and the bullet points below, which are taken from pages 236–242 of the *CFH:*

- The Ten Commandments were given to God's Chosen People, the Israelites, as a sign of their special relationship with God. They symbolized the law, which if lived faithfully would lead them to holiness. But the law was meant for everyone.
- We are able to understand the truth God revealed in those commandments because they are based on the natural law God has implanted in every person's heart. But sometimes we ignore that natural law. So God revealed the Ten Commandments to Moses to make his truth clearer.
- The Ten Commandments cover a lot of territory in teaching us how to be in right relationship with God, our neighbors, and all creation. We are able to live out these laws by the grace of God, who is always with us, loving us and nurturing us so that we can live as the people we were created to be—human beings made in God's image.
- The first three commandments concern the love of God. The next seven commandments concern love of neighbor. These commands are inseparable. We can't love God unless we love our neighbor, and the opposite is also true.

TryThis

By referring to the types of items that are false gods, as described in *The Catholic Faith Handbook for Youth,* p. 238, invite the participants to make a list of the things they own that represent false gods or that are superstitious in nature. Ask them to consider giving up such items. You might decide to conduct a collection of them sometime during the next few weeks.

TryThis

Invite the participants to discuss ways they can rework their daily schedule to allow more time for prayer, Scripture reading, or other activities to improve their relationship with God. Consider posting the ideas in your parish bulletin to benefit the entire community.

- The first commandment is a summons—a call for us to believe, to hope, and to love God above all else. It comes first because it is the basis for our life and happiness.
- This commandment also tells us that we must adore God, pray to God, and offer worship that belongs to God alone.
- Worshiping, adoring, and praying to God may sound pretty basic, but as a young person in the world today, you face competing voices about whom and what to worship. Most of us cannot imagine worshiping a golden calf, yet we may idolize the false gods of power, pleasure, popularity, or money. To idolize these things or anything else is idolatry, a sin against the first commandment. It is making them more important in our life than God.
- God calls each one of us by name. Everyone's name is sacred. It demands respect as a sign of the dignity of the one who bears it. God's name is no different, and indeed, should be treated with even more respect.
- All too often we hear people use the expressions, "Oh, God!" "Jesus Christ!" or even "Holy mother of God!" as a way to express humor, surprise, or anger. Rarely is it a situation in which people really intend to call on our God and Savior! To speak in vain means that what we say has no positive result or real value.
- With its origins in the Jewish observance of the Sabbath, Sunday has become the day of rest for Christians. Sunday is also when Christians celebrate the day of Christ's Resurrection, and so Sunday is known as the Lord's Day.
- If God rested and was refreshed, we too ought to rest and encourage others to take a day of rest. There is no denying that finding time to honor the Lord's Day can be a challenge. All that activity—studying, working, extracurricular activities—can make a person tired and weary. This is not what God intended. We need to set aside time to pray and play. Time to worship our God and leisure time are fundamental human rights.

7. Given what has been discussed so far, invite the participants to review their priority lists. Ask them to consider whether their schedule and priorities on Sunday are any different than on any other day. Ask them to review how they use God's name on an average day. Invite them to judge whether their use of God's name is respectful and prayerful.

8. Close by inviting the participants to review their habits and to plan some changes that will allow God to be not only present but a priority in their life. Allow a few minutes for them to work on their sheets. Then ask for one or two participants to give an example of how they are going to make a change (or changes) to put God first.

Conclude by noting that the content of this session was drawn from chapter 24 of the *CFH*. Encourage the participants to read and review it in the next few days.

Session Extensions

The Power of Proclaiming a Name (20 minutes)

Preparation
- Gather the following items:
  - ❏ newsprint
  - ❏ marker
  - ❏ *Catholic Youth Bible*s or other Bibles, one for each participant
  - ❏ *The Catholic Faith Handbook for Youth (CFH),* one for each participant

1. Begin by asking the participants for examples of situations when people say their name. You may want to provide a few examples or prompts, such as: "When do your teachers say your name? When do your friends say your name?"

2. Explain that when we say someone's name, we do two things. First, we call the person's attention to something. Second, we convey our feelings or our message in the way we say the name.

3. Write the following scenarios on newsprint:
- Your teacher at school is trying to get your attention when you are talking during class.
- Your younger sister, brother, niece, or nephew is saying your name to get you to play a game.
- Your mom or dad is talking to you about the fact that you didn't clean your room as requested numerous times.
- Someone is saying your name to announce you as the winner of a big sporting event or artistic competition.
- You are upset about an argument with a friend, and a family member is trying to comfort you.

4. Ask for volunteers to stand up in place and demonstrate how the speaker would say the person's name in each of these instances. Consider having different participants demonstrate the same scenario to provide variety and to enable everyone to have an opportunity to speak. Let any participants who do not want to stand up and do this exercise observe and make notes of how the other participants pronounce the name.

5. After several participants have proclaimed the person's name in the different scenarios, ask the group to share any observations they have about how the names were said. Use the following questions to spur discussion:

Media connections

- Watch some reality television this week (anything from an entertainment show to a home decorating show). Notice how many times the participants use the word *God.* Are they reflecting the respect due to God's name in the moments when they use it? Notice whether you do the same thing habitually. Can you work to break that habit?
- Check out the prayer Web site by the Irish Jesuits, *www.jesuit.ie/prayer/ index.htm,* for a new way to spend some time with God every day.
- *Old Turtle,* by Douglas Wood (New York: Scholastic Press, 1992), is a delightful children's story that tells of Creation's arguing over who or what God is. Only Old Turtle has the wisdom and the ability to see beyond herself and to incorporate what everyone has said. Read the story, and then engage the participants in a discussion of their image of God.

- Can you tell when you are in trouble just by how someone says your name? How does that make you feel?
- Can you tell when someone is angry or upset by how the person says your name? How does that make you feel?
- How would someone who is happy with you or proud of you say your name? How does that make you feel?
- Which of these scenarios makes you feel good about yourself and your relationship with the person who is saying your name?

6. Next ask the participants how this activity relates to our use of God's name when we pray to, talk about, or curse God. Help them make the connection with the obligation to use God's name in a way that expresses the joy, love, and respect that we have for God and that God has for us. Explain that we need to be aware of the message that we send to others and to God when we use God's name in vain. We wouldn't want people to associate our name with anger, disappointment, or frustration; nor does God want people to use the name of God in such a manner.

7. Instruct the group to read silently or have various participants read aloud the section in the *CFH,* pages 240–241, on the Second Commandment. Invite any insights or questions they might have after reading this section.

8. Conclude by praying together the prayer in the article "Tripping Over My Tongue," near Matt. 12:33–37, in the *CYB.*

Morality Play (20 minutes)

Preparation

- Gather the following item:
  - ❑ index cards, one for each participant

1. Prior to the arrival of the group, write the name of a vice or a virtue on each index card. You will need enough cards for each participant to have one; consider making a few extra in case you have any visitors. The same name of a vice or a virtue can appear several times, but be sure to represent a variety of virtues and vices. Consider using the following list:
- Vices: greed, envy, pride, sloth, deceit, gluttony
- Virtues: charity, humility, honesty, self-control, patience, kindness

2. Explain to the participants that as a group, they are going to perform small morality plays to portray the role that false gods play in their life, the temptations they face, and the virtues that strengthen them to do the right thing.

3. Give a simple explanation about morality plays, using the following description:

3. Then say:

- Our prayer today helps us reflect on keeping the first commandment. I will read questions aloud from the handout and allow you some time to reflect prayerfully on your response. The handout has space for you to record your answers. What you write on the handout is for your eyes only; you will not be asked to share it with anyone. Introduce the first set of reflection questions on handout 10 as follows:

- When choosing to do something, we consider time, money, and the effect the decision will have on others, including our family and friends. But do we seek God's guidance? Do we consider what God wants us to do? We know the values God wants us to live by: love, kindness, honesty, and respect for creation.

- Turn to handout 10, and respond to the reflection questions under the heading "About my choices."

Allow a few minutes for the participants to complete their answers.

4. Continue with the reflection questions as follows:

- How we display our attitudes and emotions says a lot about the presence of God in our life. Do we recognize the presence of God when we're sad as well as when we're overjoyed?

- On handout 10, respond to the reflection questions under the heading "About my attitudes and emotions."

Allow a few minutes for the participants to complete their answers.

5. Continue with the reflection questions as follows:

- Paying attention to our prayer life is essential in our relationship with God. Does our prayer focus on asking God to help us see our true needs and meet those needs? How can we base our prayer on our love for God?

- On handout 10, respond to the reflection questions under the heading "About my prayer life."

Allow a few minutes for the participants to complete their answers.

6. Continue with the reflection questions as follows:

- Our relationships with other people include God. Do we treat others as God intends? How do our interactions show the presence of God?

- On handout 10, respond to the reflection questions under the heading "About my relationships."

Allow a few minutes for the participants to complete their answers. Then say:

- We have spent some time reflecting on the first commandment and on how we try to keep God first in our life.

- We recognize the temptations all around us that make it difficult to make God "number one."

- We acknowledge the good efforts we make every day to keep focused on what is important and to remember God's gift of love for us.

Familyconnections

- Suggest that each participant's family discuss its priorities. How are each member's priorities similar or different? How will the family's free time be spent: vacuuming the carpet or going on a picnic? surfing the Internet or going on a bike ride? What is important for the family?

- Suggest that each participant's family members share their image of God with one another, perhaps by making a collage of magazine pictures and words to create a family image of God.

- Send home a shoebox covered in white paper with a question written on each side of the box. Invite the participant's family to have a discussion based on one of the questions. Include questions such as: How did you experience God today? How do you experience God in nature? in music? with your friends? at work?

TryThis

Consider using the Pray It article "Avoiding False Gods," on page 238 in *The Catholic Faith Handbook for Youth,* as an alternative or an addition to the prayer service.

- By offering a prayer of petition, we ask for God's strength to help us say yes to his invitation of love. After each prayer, our response will be "God, strengthen us."

Invite the participants to offer a prayer of petition. If the group is shy or unsure of what you expect from them, begin the prayer yourself, or use the following prayer:

- God, for the times when I do not recognize your presence in my daily life, please grant me new eyes to see more clearly. We pray to the Lord.

7. In closing, play or sing the song you have chosen. Encourage the group to put God first in every way by saying to themselves, "Lord, this is for you."

Options and Actions

- **God's presence.** Gather current magazines or newspapers. Invite the participants to cut out examples of God's presence in the world today. Talk about the various ways, which are sometimes difficult to see, in which God is present to us, showing love and concern for all people. Place these examples in a gift-wrapped box, and offer a prayer of thanksgiving to God.
- **Cinquain** *(sin-kane).* Create a simple five-line poem by using the following formula:
  - ○ one word as title of the poem
  - ○ two words describing the title
  - ○ three words showing action
  - ○ four words telling how you feel about the subject
  - ○ another word for the title

    Use "God" as the title of the poem. Here is a sample using another title:

Children
fun alive
laughing loving playing
precious in God's sight
Gift

- **Symbols of faith.** Gather a variety of old household items. Try to have at least one item for each person. Ask a volunteer to read 2 Tim. 2:20–26 to the group. Invite each person to select an item and to think about how it can symbolize his or her relationship with God.
- **Bookmarks.** Gather bibles, strips of construction paper (2½ inches by 8½ inches) in various colors, colored gel pens (not markers) or other pens, and Christian or other appropriate stickers. Invite all the participants to create bookmarks that will encourage their relationship with God. Suggest that they locate a brief Scripture passage as the key thought for their bookmarks.

Honoring God

This session covers pages 236–244 of *The Catholic Faith Handbook for Youth*. For further exploration, check out paragraph numbers 2052–2195 of the *Catechism of the Catholic Church*.

Session Summary

- The Ten Commandments were given to God's Chosen People, the Israelites, as a sign of their special relationship with God. They symbolized the law, which if lived faithfully would lead them to holiness. But the law was meant for everyone.

- We are able to understand the truth God revealed in those commandments because they are based on the natural law God has implanted in every person's heart. But sometimes we ignore that natural law. So God revealed the Ten Commandments to Moses to make his truth clearer.

- The Ten Commandments cover a lot of territory in teaching us how to be in right relationship with God, our neighbors, and all creation. We are able to live out these laws by the grace of God, who is always with us, loving us and nurturing us so that we can live as the people we were created to be—human beings made in God's image.

- The first three commandments concern the love of God. The next seven commandments concern love of neighbor. These commands are inseparable. We can't love God unless we love our neighbor, and the opposite is also true.

- The first commandment is a summons—a call for us to believe, to hope, and to love God above all else. It comes first because it is the basis for our life and happiness.

- This commandment also tells us that we must adore God, pray to God, and offer worship that belongs to God alone.

- Worshiping, adoring, and praying to God may sound pretty basic, but as a young person in the world today, you face competing voices about who and what to worship. Most of us cannot imagine worshiping a golden calf, yet we may idolize the false gods of power, pleasure, popularity, or money. To idolize these things or anything else is idolatry, a sin against the first commandment. It is making them more important in our life than God.

- God calls each one of us by name. Everyone's name is sacred. It demands respect as a sign of the dignity of the one who bears it. God's name is no different, and indeed, should be treated with even more respect.
- All too often we hear people use the expressions, "Oh, God!" "Jesus Christ!" or even "Holy mother of God!" as a way to express humor, surprise, or anger. Rarely is it a situation in which people really intend to call on our God and Savior! To speak in vain means that what we say has no positive result or real value.
- With its origins in the Jewish observance of the Sabbath, Sunday has become the day of rest for Christians. Sunday is also when Christians celebrate the day of Christ's Resurrection, and so Sunday is the known as the Lord's Day.
- If God rested and was refreshed, we too ought to rest and encourage others to take a day of rest. There is no denying that finding time to honor the Lord's Day can be a challenge. All that activity—studying, working, extracurricular activities—can make a person tired and weary. This is not what God intended. We need to set aside time to pray and play. Time to worship our God and leisure time are fundamental human rights.

(All summary points are taken from *The Catholic Faith Handbook for Youth,* by Brian Singer-Towns et al. [Winona, MN: Saint Mary's Press, 2004], pages 236–242. Copyright © 2004 by Saint Mary's Press. All rights reserved.)

Talk Points

- Who is God for you? What images best describe God for you? Have these images changed since you were young? How?
- Does anyone you know value God in his or her life? How do you know this to be true?
- State the first commandment in your own words. Does restating it make it more meaningful to you? How?
- How can prayer help you improve your relationship with God?
- After God, what are your top three priorities in life?
- Besides God, to whom must you be obedient? How is this obedience the same as or different from being obedient to God?

Lord, This Is for You

Reflecting on the first commandment

About my choices . . . Recall a decision you made recently. In making this decision, did you rank God first in the process? last? Did you consider God in making this decision? Why or why not?

About my attitudes and emotions . . . Think of someone you don't really care for. Just as you are created in the image and likeness of God, so is this person. God loves you both equally. Are you humble enough to recognize God in this person? What is one thing you can do for or say to this person?

About my prayer life . . . Think about the past few weeks. Has God been your focus in prayer? What have you been praying for or about? Have you focused your prayer on what you want or on God's help in discerning what you truly need? What is one thing you can say to God in prayer that shows your love of God?

About my relationships . . . God is always with you. Do you live as if this statement were true? In your relationships with others, do you treat them as if God were standing next to you? In talking with others, are you aware of God's presence?

5 Honoring Family
An Intergenerational Session

Overview

The first three commandments concern our relationship with God; the rest, our relationship with our neighbor. The fourth commandment focuses on our relationship with our closest neighbor, our parents, and by extension, other family members and authorities. Young people need to understand the relationship between God and their parents or people who are in the role of parents. This session involves young people and their parents in exploring the parental relationship and the responsibilities and love that flow between parents and children. In addition, the session expands the parent-child relationship to include our relationship with civil authorities and the Church's relationship with those authorities. In preparing this session, be aware that not all participants come from an ideal family situation. Take special care to be sensitive to this and to adjust the session content accordingly. If parent participation is limited, consider conducting the session with just the young people.

Outcomes

- The learner will appreciate that God is the source of the mutual respect due within the family.
- The learner will understand the relationship between the child's responsibility of respect and the parent's duty of care.
- The learner will understand how the fourth commandment applies to the civil authority.
- The learner will understand that civil disobedience and political action are based on Catholic teachings.

Study It

Core Session
- Advertising for the Ideal Society
  (45 minutes)

Session Extensions
- When We Disobey
  (20 minutes)
- Standing Up for Human Dignity
  (25 minutes)

Pray It
- Growing in Family Respect
  (20 minutes)

Live It
- Setting an example
- Get involved
- People watching
- Parental joy

73

Background Reading

◆ This session covers pages 245–252 of *The Catholic Faith Handbook for Youth*.

◆ For further exploration, check out paragraph numbers 2197–2257 of the *Catechism*.

◆ Scriptural connections: Prov. 30:17 (on mocking and disobeying parents), Sir. 3:1–16 (duties toward parents), Eph. 5:21—6:4 (the Christian household), Col. 3:20—4:1 ("Children, obey your parents.")

◆ *Catholic Youth Bible* article connections: "Ravens and Vultures" (Prov. 30:17), "Honoring Our Parents in God's Way" (Sir. 3:1–16), "Introducing the Holy Family" (Luke 2:41–52), "Restrain Your Ego" (1 Cor. 8:1–13), "Family Relationships" (Eph. 5:12—6:4), "The Christian Family" (Col. 3:20—4:1)

Core Session

Advertising for the Ideal Society (45 minutes)

Preparation

• Gather the following items:
  ❑ copies of handout 11, "Honoring Family: An Intergenerational Session," one for each participant
  ❑ copies of *The Catholic Faith Handbook for Youth (CFH),* one for every participant
  ❑ sheets of colored and white paper
  ❑ pens, pencils, thick- and thin-line markers, scissors, glue sticks, and any other art supplies you might have on hand
  ❑ newsprint

• Review the summary points in step 3 of this session and the relevant material on pages 245–249 of the *CFH*. Be prepared to share the information with the young people.

1. Begin by dividing the participants into four groups. If you are conducting this session with both young people and parents, be sure to have a good mix of both in each small group. Set up the activity with the following details:

- Tell the participants that they are now the principal creative minds at the top four advertising agencies in the city of Ideal. Ideal is a place where all the inhabitants can choose who their parents are, who their children are, and who their civic leaders are. The civic leaders even get to choose what kind of community they will lead.
- Ask the participants to think about what they know about advertising, based on the ads they've seen and heard throughout their life.
- Remind them that people who create ads know their product (what they are selling), their market (to whom they are selling), and the successful ideas that are occurring with similar markets and products.
- Inform the participants that you will tell them what product they will be selling and who will be buying it. You will present the facts that will be useful to them in selling their various products. They should pay careful attention to the presentation.

2. Assign one of the following advertising jobs to each of the four groups; two groups will be advertising parents, and two groups will be advertising children:
- Advertising children to prospective parents
- Advertising parents to prospective children

3. Conduct a presentation on honoring family, using the bullet points below, which are taken from pages 245–249 of the *CFH*. Remind the participants to pay attention because they will need the information later. Before you begin, let them know that the beliefs and values of the citizens of Ideal are the same as those that the Catholic Church teaches.
- We don't get to choose our family ties, but the bonds that we share with the members of our family last a lifetime, for better or for worse. In the best of times, parents, children, and siblings enjoy and support one another. This brings us to the fourth commandment, "Honor your father and your mother." As is true with all the commandments, it is about more than just your relationship with your parents.
- Focusing on the responsibilities and duties that family members have toward one another is the first step in knowing how we are to act toward all people.
- The fourth commandment is based on this natural love between parent and child that God has placed in the human heart.
- Even though the fourth commandment is addressed toward children instead of parents, the Church teaches that it implies moral responsibilities that go both ways.
- The Church defines the duties of this commandment as attitudes that lead to specific actions. The Church teaches that the attitudes children owe parents are respect, gratitude, obedience, and assistance.

JournalACTIVITIES

- If you were to create the perfect community, what would it look like? Who would be part of the community? How would you and the other members agree to live as a community?
- Mutual respect within the family cannot happen without a measure of self-respect. How do you define the term *self-respect?*
- Imagine yourself as a person who is of a race, a group, or a culture different from your own. Who would respect this person's human dignity and who would not? How would it feel to be in this person's shoes?

- In a similar way, God gives parents the responsibility to teach their children about God and the moral life and to make rules for your safety—even if it means telling you things you would rather not hear.
- Not only must parents provide for the physical, emotional, and spiritual needs of their children (those things you should be grateful for), but they must also be your first educators, especially when it comes to your faith life.
- As you grow older, the natural progression that God created requires that parents give you more freedom as you make your own choices. This can be very hard for some parents to do.

4. Remind each group what its advertising job is, and recall that Ideal, true to its name, is an ideal city: people can choose their parents or their children. Encourage each small group to make its "product" look good to the target market by showing how the product fulfills the beliefs and values about the family. The group members should decide what the best features of their Ideal children or parents are. What will make them most attractive to the Ideal parents or children to whom they are selling? Suggest that the groups take a few minutes to talk about their product and their market before creating the ads.

5. Write on newsprint the following attributes that the people of Ideal value in their children and in their parents:
- Children: respect, gratitude, obedience, assistance
- Parents: responsibility; safety; physical, emotional, and spiritual security

The groups need to highlight these attributes in the ad campaign. You can also take this opportunity to brainstorm with the large group other desirable attributes in a child or a parent, based on the presentation you just gave.

6. When the groups are ready to create the ads, show them the art supplies, and invite them to take what they need and to share as necessary. They can create ad campaigns using any combination of formats: billboard, television, radio, newspaper and magazines, catalogues, the Web. They can work as one group, or the members can split off individually or in groups of two to handle smaller pieces of the campaign. Give the groups 15 minutes to produce the ad campaign.

7. When done, each group will present its ad campaign to the rest of the participants. When each group finishes presenting, ask the participants whether and why they are attracted to the product being sold.

8. When all four groups have finished, ask the participants to talk about the similarities and the differences between the Ideal children and parents, as advertised, and what their own experience has been. Be certain to welcome comments from both perspectives and to encourage the parents and the young people to speak with mutual respect and consideration.

9. If time allows, help the participants relate this topic to the roles and responsibilities of civil authorities and the members of a community. For this discussion, use the section titled "Responsibilities of Civil Authorities," on pages 249–250 of the *CFH*.

10. Close the session by inviting the young people to reconnect with their parents and to choose and discuss one aspect of the advertised Ideal children and parents that they will try to live up to. Be sure to note that the content of this session was drawn from chapter 25 of the *CFH*. Encourage the participants to read and review it in the next few days.

Session Extensions

When We Disobey (20 minutes)

Preparation
- Gather the following items:
  - ❏ a *Catholic Youth Bible* or other Bible, opened to Luke 2:41–51
  - ❏ newsprint
  - ❏ masking tape
  - ❏ markers
  - ❏ paper
  - ❏ pens or pencils
- Review the story of Jesus in the Temple in Luke 2:41–51.
- Tape three sheets of newsprint to the wall. Label them "Physical Harm," "Emotional Harm," and "Spiritual Harm."

1. Begin by distributing paper and pens or pencils to the participants. Instruct them to make two columns. Ask them to list in the lefthand column five situations in which young people might be tempted to disobey their parents. If parents are participating, have the young people group with their parents to create this list.

2. Once the participants have completed their lists, ask the young people to identify (for each of the five situations listed) the potential danger or harm that the parents were so concerned about that they forbade or required something directly related to whatever the participants (or friends) were tempted to disobey. The participants should list these harms in the right-hand column.

3. Have the participants name some of the specific harms or dangers on the list that the parents were most concerned about. Write these harms on the newsprint under the appropriate heading.

4. Invite the participants to share the reasons why young people are tempted to disobey and to explain how those reasons might outweigh the risk and the harm that the parents are most concerned about.

5. Ask one participant to read Luke 2:41–51. Have the group discuss Jesus' disobedience in the context of the risk-benefit analysis they just did when discussing disobedience. Consider these questions: How might a young person's reason for disobeying compare with Jesus' reason for disobeying (to be in the Temple, the house of God, his Father, talking about the Law with the teachers)? How does the risk Jesus faced compare with the risks from which parents today are trying to protect their children from? How does the fact that Jesus was obedient for the rest of his life compare with what parents might expect from their children?

6. Explain that just because we disagree with a rule or an expectation a parent might have for us, we do not have the right to disobey and to ignore what our parents ask. We ought to reflect on what they are trying to teach us or protect us from. When we understand the motivation behind the rule or expectation, we are more likely to see the positive impact it will have on us as we grow up.

7. Close the activity by inviting the participants to consider that they have a duty to obey their parents, who have a responsibility to care for them. If young people think they can "make a case" for why a rule should be changed, they should raise the issue at a time when nothing will interfere with a calm discussion.

Standing Up for Human Dignity (25 minutes)

Preparation
- Gather the following items:
  - ❑ newsprint
  - ❑ markers
  - ❑ copies of *The Catholic Faith Handbook for Youth (CFH),* one for each group of four participants
- Review the material in the sections "Responsibilities of Civil Authorities" and "Church and State" and in the article "Civil Disobedience," on pages 249–252 of the *CFH.*

1. Begin by inviting the participants to complete the statement, "We have laws because . . ." Write their responses on the newsprint.

2. Then ask the participants to express the similarities between parents and civil authorities. Be sure to point out aspects such as these:

- They look out for our well-being.
- They establish rules that we are supposed to live by.
- They look at the big picture rather than what will bring immediate gratification.

3. Next divide the participants into groups of four or five. Have the groups brainstorm any civil laws with which they don't agree and the reasons why they disagree. Have them record their ideas on newsprint. You can give a few examples, such as the drinking age, the speed limit, and mandatory seatbelt laws. Give the groups approximately 5 minutes for this part of the activity.

4. Encourage each group to share its list with the large group. Be sure that any law they disagree with also has a reason for this disagreement. You can list on newsprint the laws with which they disagree.

5. Follow the listing of laws with a discussion about what makes a law just or unjust. Explain that a law is unjust if it is morally wrong, and that we know what is morally right and wrong through natural law, the Scriptures, and the Tradition of the Church.

6. Ask the participants to look again at the list of laws with which they disagree and to decide whether those laws are morally wrong or just something with which they disagree. For example, speed limits are not morally wrong; they serve the greater purpose of keeping people safe. Disagreeing with a law does not make the law morally wrong.

7. Invite the participants to brainstorm the laws, situations, world events, or activities that Catholics oppose but that some governments support. They can cite ones that you have already introduced from the *CFH,* such as segregation, abortion, and the death penalty. As criteria for judging whether a law is morally wrong, have them consider whether the law values human life and respects the dignity of the person, the importance of the family, and care for the environment. This subject is difficult and emotionally charged, so be sure to stress that we are not debating the issues raised; instead, we are bringing to light a challenging aspect of our faith and our life in the larger community. Summarize their ideas on newsprint.

8. After you have listed issues that Catholics oppose but that some governments support, have the small groups come up with ways they can voice opposition to these laws. Allow the groups about 5 minutes for this part of the activity.

9. When you have gathered everyone back into the large group, give the small groups an opportunity to report a few of their ideas. Take care not to dismiss any ideas; at the same time, be sure to address any suggestions

Mediaconnections

◆ Consider using a portion of the movie *Freaky Friday* (Disney, 93 minutes, 2003, rated PG) to illustrate the need to look at things from the perspective of our parents as well as from our own perspective. The 2003 version of this film is popular with young people and provides a good connection between the subject matter and their life.

◆ *The Long Walk Home* (Miramax, 97 minutes, 1990, rated PG), starring Whoopi Goldberg and Sissy Spacek, illustrates the effect of the 1955 bus boycott led by Martin Luther King Jr. on the lives of two women. The film is a wonderful exploration of the everyday cost of opposing a morally unjust law.

◆ Select an episode of a popular family television drama or comedy. Show a scene, and then analyze whether each member of the family is respecting the others. At the end, add up the assessments to determine whether this program ultimately leans toward mutual respect or an imbalance, one way or the other. Ask the participants whether they would like to emulate this family.

they bring up that advocate violence or compromise one belief to protect another.

10. After the small groups have reported their ideas about how people can oppose laws and actions that are morally wrong, be sure to stress the following points, which are taken from page 250 of the *CFH:*

- We must work together with our leaders to build up the moral environment of the world we live in, making it easier to be good.
- Our actions and attitudes must contribute to the good of society in a spirit of truth, justice, solidarity, and freedom.
- Just as you must obey your parents unless you believe their expectations are morally wrong, so you must also obey the laws of your community.
- Not every law is morally right. If we have good reasons to believe a law is morally wrong, then the opposite is true. We are obliged not to follow it. Refusing to follow immoral laws is called civil disobedience.

11. Wrap up this activity by making the following point:

- As people of faith, we are called to act on behalf of our faith by speaking and acting against laws that are morally wrong. Civil disobedience is one method, but only after we have exhausted all legal ways to change the law or the action that is morally wrong.

If time allows, consider having the participants read the article "Civil Disobedience," on page 249 of the *CFH,* and share any reflections they might have.

12. Close by inviting the participants to stay attentive to these issues in their life and to consider what action they want to take in response to them.

Growing in Family Respect (20 minutes)

Preparation
- Gather the following items:
  - ❑ a prayer table
  - ❑ a candle and matches
  - ❑ smooth, polished stones, one for each participant
  - ❑ a basket large enough to hold all the stones
  - ❑ a *Catholic Youth Bible* or other Bible, opened to Eph. 3:14–19

❏ copies of resource 2, "Growing as Family," one for every two participants
❏ a tape player or a CD player
❏ a song with a family theme
• Copy resource 2, and cut it in half as scored.
• Light the candle; place it and the basket in the center of the prayer table.
  Place the polished stones in the basket.

1. Begin by calling the group to prayer. Ask them to form a circle. In your own words, invite the participants to reflect on the discussion and on the activities they have experienced in this session. After recalling the key points, make the following comment:
• Now we take time to thank God for the blessings of those people in our life who are our family: parents, sons, daughters, brothers, sisters, and all who care deeply for us.

2. Ask a volunteer to proclaim the Scripture reading, Eph. 3:14–19. Allow a few minutes of reflection.

3. Tell the participants that developing good relationships within the family takes time and hard work. Pick up one of the polished stones, and say:
• This stone was once rough around the edges, but through time and effort it is now smooth. The same is true of us. As we learn and experience more of life in the love of God and family, our rough edges become smoother.
• Each of us will receive a smooth stone as a reminder that every day we get better at developing relationships within our family; we get smoother around the edges.

4. Call one of the participants to the center of the circle. Select a polished stone from the basket, and give it to the person as a challenge to work on developing good relationships within his or her family. Say:
• Receive this stone as a reminder of the person you are becoming because of and with your family.
The recipient, in turn, calls another participant to the circle and gives him or her a stone, repeating the same phrase, "Receive this stone as a reminder of the person you are becoming because of and with your family." Repeat the process until all have received a stone.

5. Distribute the half-sheet copies of resource 2, and invite the participants to pray the prayer together. Have them offer one another a sign of God's peace. Close the prayer with your chosen song.

Familyconnections

◆ Suggest that the participants assess their awareness of their parents' views on moral issues and identify the issues that they would like to discuss more extensively with their parents. Perhaps some issues provide common ground or mutual interest around which parents and children can unite to improve the larger community.

◆ Suggest that families make a list of the ways they can respect one another on a daily basis. What is the bare minimum necessary for a family to live together in mutual respect and harmony?

◆ Suggest that families brainstorm the qualities of a good parent and a good child. Parents and children can give themselves a report card on how they are doing and make a commitment to spend the next month (or year) trying to improve on an issue.

Options and Actions

- **Setting an example.** Look in the Scriptures for examples of families that faced difficulty in different ways. Examples include Abraham being asked to sacrifice Isaac (Gen. 22:1–9), Joseph and his brothers (Gen., chap. 37), Naomi and Ruth (Ruth 1:6–18), Hosea and his wife Gomer (Hos. 3:1–3), and Mary and Jesus at Cana (John 2:1–11). What was the nature of the family? What strengthened it? What weakened it? What can these examples teach us about dealing with our own family?

- **Get involved.** One way to live out our community responsibility is to help others. Provide the participants with a list of service opportunities available to them: volunteer work at a soup kitchen, in an after-school program for children, at a shelter for homeless children, in your parish religious education program, and so forth. How is the local civic authority trying to serve these people? Is it succeeding?

- **People watching.** Suggest that the participants spend some time observing people in public places (a library, a shopping center, a park, and so forth). Ask them to reflect on the question, What can you tell about various families by observing them together?

- **Parental joy.** Have the young people ask their parents (or primary caregiver) to talk about what their hopes and dreams and thoughts were when they were expecting the participant and what it was like right after she or he came into their lives. Even if the participants have heard the stories before, invite them to listen with openness this time and to look for the reflection of God's love in the way the parent-child relationship began.

Honoring Family: An Intergenerational Session

This session covers pages 245–252 of *The Catholic Faith Handbook for Youth*. For further exploration, check out paragraph numbers 2197–2257 of the *Catechism of the Catholic Church*.

Session Summary

- We don't get to choose our family ties, but the bonds that we share with the members of our family last a lifetime, for better or for worse. In the best of times, parents, children, and siblings enjoy and support one another. This brings us to the fourth commandment, "Honor your father and your mother." As is true with all the commandments, it is about more than just your relationship with your parents.

- Focusing on the responsibilities and duties that family members have toward one another is the first step in knowing how we are to act toward all people.

- The fourth commandment is based on this natural love between parent and child that God has placed in the human heart.

- Even though the fourth commandment is addressed toward children instead of parents, the Church teaches that it implies moral responsibilities that go both ways.

- The Church defines the duties of this commandment as attitudes that lead to specific actions. The Church teaches that the attitudes children owe parents are respect, gratitude, obedience, and assistance.

- In a similar way, God gives parents the responsibility to teach their children about God and the moral life and to make rules for your safety— even if it means telling you things you would rather not hear.

- Not only must parents provide for the physical, emotional, and spiritual needs of their children (those things you should be grateful for), but they must also be your first educators, especially when it comes to your faith life.

- As you grow older, the natural progression that God created requires that parents give you more freedom as you make your own choices. This can be very hard for some parents to do.

- We must work together with our leaders to build up the moral environment of the world we live in, making it easier to be good.

- Our actions and attitudes must contribute to the good of society in a spirit of truth, justice, solidarity, and freedom.
- Just as you must obey your parents unless you believe their expectations are morally wrong, so you must also obey the laws of your community.
- Not every law is morally right. If we have good reasons to believe a law is morally wrong, then the opposite is true. We are obliged *not* to follow it. Refusing to follow immoral laws is called civil disobedience.

(All summary points are taken from *The Catholic Faith Handbook for Youth,* by Brian Singer-Towns et al. [Winona, MN: Saint Mary's Press, 2004], pages 245–250. Copyright © 2004 by Saint Mary's Press. All rights reserved.)

Talk Points

- Make a list of everyday activities in which you participate. Then talk about the people or institutions on which these activities depend.
- Talk about why it is not possible to "go it alone" in life.

Growing as Family

Dear Jesus,

Thank you for my family. They want the best for me, even if we sometimes disagree on what that is. They support me in countless ways—many I'm probably not even aware of. They do their best to be agents of your love in my life. I try to give them the love and respect they deserve.

Spirit of Jesus, watch over my family just as you watch over me. Show them your loving acceptance and support. Help them to look honestly at themselves and at the decisions they are making and to keep the best interests of the family always in mind. When they experience pain, frustration, or failure, give them strength to lean on you. Fill their days with laughter and love. Protect and keep them safe all the days of their lives. Amen.

(This prayer is adapted from the article "A Prayer for Friends," near John 18:6 in *The Catholic Youth Bible,* first edition [Winona, MN: Saint Mary's Press, 2000]. Copyright © 2000 by Saint Mary's Press. All rights reserved.)

--✂

Dear Jesus,

Thank you for my family. They want the best for me, even if we sometimes disagree on what that is. They support me in countless ways—many I'm probably not even aware of. They do their best to be agents of your love in my life. I try to give them the love and respect they deserve.

Spirit of Jesus, watch over my family just as you watch over me. Show them your loving acceptance and support. Help them to look honestly at themselves and at the decisions they are making and to keep the best interests of the family always in mind. When they experience pain, frustration, or failure, give them strength to lean on you. Fill their days with laughter and love. Protect and keep them safe all the days of their lives. Amen.

(This prayer is adapted from the article "A Prayer for Friends," near John 18:6 in *The Catholic Youth Bible,* first edition [Winona, MN: Saint Mary's Press, 2000]. Copyright © 2000 by Saint Mary's Press. All rights reserved.)

--✂

Respecting Life

Overview

The fifth commandment can come across to young people as being narrow in scope. This session explores the breadth of the fifth commandment in relation to various life issues and to responsibility for personal life and health. In addition, the chapter stresses the underlying rationale of the fifth commandment.

Outcomes

◆ The learner will recognize that the foundation of the fifth commandment is the fact that all humans are created in the image of God.

◆ The learner will understand how life issues—such as capital punishment, war, abortion, genetic engineering, euthanasia, suicide, and scandal—are related to the fifth commandment.

◆ The learner will realize that the responsibility to respect life includes respecting her or his own health.

Background Reading

◆ This session covers pages 253–264 of *The Catholic Faith Handbook for Youth*.

◆ For further exploration, check out paragraph numbers 2258–2330 of the *Catechism*.

◆ Scriptural connections: Deut. 30:15,19 (choosing life), Ps. 139:13–16 (the inescapable God), Luke 4:16–21 (Jesus teaching in the Temple)

◆ *Catholic Youth Bible* article connections: "The Cycle of Violence" (Gen. 4:15), "The Sacredness of Life" (Psalm 139), "We Are God's Temple" (1 Cor. 3:16–17)

Core Session

Life Is . . . (45 minutes)

Preparation

- Gather the following items:
  - ❏ copies of handout 12, "Respecting Life," one for each participant
  - ❏ sheets of blank paper, one for each participant
  - ❏ pens or pencils
- Review the summary points in step 8 of this session and the relevant material on pages 253–264 of *The Catholic Faith Handbook for Youth (CFH)*. Be prepared to share the information with the young people.
- This topic has the potential to be difficult for young people, particularly if they have experienced personal situations of life and death. Prior to the session, you may want to touch base with your director of religious education or coordinator of youth ministry on how to deal with any situations that might arise.

1. Begin by sharing with the participants that this session will explore some tough issues that face us as individuals and as a society. It is important to remember that we all have different experiences that we bring to our gathering. We gather to explore and to deepen our faith in God through the truths that the Church teaches. Let the participants know that if they have questions or issues they would like to talk about in more detail following the session, you will be available or will assist them in finding the right person to speak with.

2. Distribute a pen or pencil and a piece of paper to each participant.

3. Explain that you are going to read a series of sentences in which the last word is missing. The participants are to write down the first word that comes to mind to complete the sentence. Ask them to use a different word for each sentence.

4. Before you start reading the sentences, have the participants number the paper 1 to 12 down the left side. They will write next to the appropriate number the word that comes to mind for each sentence. Explain that this exercise is to be done individually and silently and that there will be time for sharing later in the session.

Familyconnections

- Invite each family member to write a note to another family member that affirms the gift the family member has shared.

- Using the family's last name, create an acrostic by using words that relate to how the family values life. (Example: J = joyful praise to God; O = openness to change; N = naming the gifts in others; S = serving in a soup kitchen)

- What gifts do children bring to your life? What gifts do older people bring to your life? Can you imagine what your life would be like if the parents of a child you are close to had aborted her or him? Can you imagine what life would be like if the last time an older person who is close to you was seriously ill, someone had chosen to end her or his life? (*CFH*, p. 264)

5. Begin reading the statements below, allowing time after each sentence for the participants to write down their responses. Read each statement a few times, and tell the participants when you are going to move to the next sentence to be completed.

- Life is . . .
- I was created because . . .
- The best thing about my life is . . .
- The biggest challenge of my life is . . .
- Life is . . .
- My life is . . .
- I see God's work in my life when . . .
- In my life I will . . .
- Life is . . .
- I see others not valuing life when . . .
- Being created in God's image means . . .
- Life is . . .

6. Invite the participants to share a few of the words they used to complete the sentences. Remind the group that we are to respect others and what they have to say, so this is not a time to debate, to laugh at, or to question what people share. Consider writing on newsprint the words the participants share.

7. After they have had a chance to share, ask them to say what words on the newsprint they think best express what life is. What words on the newsprint do they like but perhaps had not thought of before?

8. Follow the discussion with a brief presentation on the theme of Catholic teaching on respecting life, using the bullet points below, which are taken from pages 253–262 of the *CFH*:

- The natural law God has put in our heart tells us that every human life has eternal value. From the unborn child to the person who has lived more than one hundred years, every life is sacred. Despite the most advanced scientific discoveries and technologies, the mystery of life and death ultimately leads us to God.

- God expects us to stand in awe of human life, to have profound respect for the dignity of the human person. The word *respect* means "to look again." But no generation before has had to consider so many complex and controversial issues that threaten the dignity of life.

- We are made in the image of God—each and every one of us. No exceptions. From the first chapter of Genesis to the most recent edition of the *Catechism,* this statement about who we are and what kind of person God wants us to be is at the heart of morality. It is the foundation for loving other people, our God, and ourselves.

- Sometimes the lives of others or even our own life may not be perfect, and life can make demands on us that are not what we want. Children and adults who are disabled or ill can require a great deal of demanding care. Sometimes other people can be annoying, inconvenient, or even our enemy. But each life is as precious to God as we are. We can never throw a life away. The beginning and end of every life is up to God, and only God.

- Although murder is clearly wrong, what about killing in self-defense? The Church teaches that we have the right to stop someone from inflicting harm on us or others. But if possible we must avoid taking the life of the one who threatens us.

- The issue of the death penalty presents a major challenge to society. The majority of the people in the United States support the use of the death penalty, also called capital punishment. Today the Church teaches that capital punishment is moral only when it is impossible to effectively defend human life in any other way. Because we have prison systems that can adequately protect society, Pope John Paul II has said that moral reasons for using the death penalty "are very rare, if not practically non-existent"[3] (CCC, number 2267). The Church recognizes that even the worst immoral act does not take away a person's God-given dignity.

- War, as an act of self-defense, is another challenging issue when we talk about respect for human life. Although armed conflict can be a valid way of protecting against unjust aggressors, we know that war brings evils and injustices to all of society. So the Church teaches that all citizens and all governments must do everything they can to avoid war.

- The reality is that war still happens, and countries must defend themselves. The principles of legitimate self-defense are just as applicable for nations as they are for individuals. However, war must be a last resort, and over the centuries the Church developed criteria that must be met if a war is morally permissible.

- One of the most controversial life issues in society today is abortion. Abortion intentionally stops the development of an unborn child. It is controversial because not everyone agrees with the Church that from conception, a child has the right to life.

- Recent scientific and technological breakthroughs show that signs of life are present long before a mother and father are aware that they have conceived a child. Science can use this information to promote respect for life, or in ways that are not so respectful. There are serious moral questions about genetic engineering, cloning, and other ways of conceiving life in ways that God did not intend.

- Moral issues exist on the other end of human life. One of those issues is euthanasia, also called mercy killing. Proponents of euthanasia make it an issue of human freedom, saying that people—or their family if the person

Mediaconnections

- As a means of exploring the secular culture's different perspectives on abortion, have the participants reflect on the meaning and the implications of some of the slogans and terms (such as pro-child, pro-choice, pro-life) that surround the debate about abortion.

- Show selected scenes from the movie *Dead Man Walking* (Metro-Goldwyn-Mayer, 122 minutes, 1995, rated R). (Obtain parental permission for the participants who are minors to view an R-rated movie, and use your best judgment regarding the appropriateness of the film and the advisability of viewing relevant excerpts.) Ask the participants to identify the various voices present in the movie. How do those voices challenge our society?

- Check out the following organizations and Web sites that promote life: Feminists for Life at *www.feministsforlife.org,* National Coalition to Abolish the Death Penalty at *www.ncadp.org,* National Teens for Life at *www.nrlc.org/outreach/teens.html.*

- Create a montage of musical excerpts or of images that illustrate the concept of the consistent life ethic.

JournalACTIVITIES

◆ This country has been involved in war in your lifetime. According to the criteria for a just war, do you think these wars are morally right? (*CFH*, p. 264)

◆ We live in a throwaway and convenience society. We easily dispose of and replace things that are no longer useful, worn out, or no longer convenient. Do you think this throwaway mentality leads to a lack of respect for human life? Why or why not? (*CFH*, pp. 263–264)

◆ How much would you be willing to give to save another person's life? Would who the person is or the circumstances of the situation affect your response?

is incapable of making their own decisions—have a right to choose to end their life. But the Church teaches that euthanasia is a serious moral wrong. The Church considers the act of intentionally causing the death of a human being to be murder, regardless of the motive or the circumstances.

• Suicide is also a grave offense against the fifth commandment. As sacred as life is, it can certainly seem overwhelming at times. But suicide, the taking of your own life, goes against human nature. As human beings, created by God, we are meant to preserve our own life as well as the lives of others. Suicide is the ultimate rejection of love of self, love of God, and love of neighbor.

• Respect for life also includes caring for the spiritual life of other people. Scandal is an attitude or behavior that deliberately leads another person to sin, causing harm to their spiritual life. Things we do, say, or wear can be scandalous. For example, offering alcohol to someone who is underage is scandalous behavior.

• The fifth commandment, "You shall not kill," also covers respect for health as part of respect for life. We are wonderfully made—body, mind, and soul. When any aspect of our being is hurting, we cannot be whole, the way God made us. As individuals we must have respect for our own health, avoiding all kinds of excess: the abuse of food, alcohol, tobacco, or drugs.

9. Ask the participants to look at their list of words to see whether it matches what we have learned from the *CFH* about the value of life.

10. Share with them that respecting and valuing life to its fullest is not always easy. Valuing the life of someone convicted of murder is difficult, for in this situation we are trying to value life while we are in great pain or are seeing those we love in pain. Valuing life, when that new life will change our life in a way we don't feel we are ready for, is a challenge. We are called, however, to work to value life at all its stages.

11. Invite the participants to revisit the statement, "Life is . . ." Ask them to write a brief letter on their piece of paper to an imaginary person who is struggling with the issue of valuing life. Possibilities could be someone who supports the death penalty, is considering an abortion, or is contemplating euthanasia. The letter should begin with the statement "Life is . . ." and explain why valuing life is necessary even when a person finds it difficult to see that value. Encourage the participants to use the *CFH* as a resource. Assure them that the letter will not be shared with the group.

12. Conclude by noting that the content of this session was drawn from chapter 26 of the *CFH*. Encourage the participants to read and review it in the next few days. Then offer the following prayer. Invite the participants to pray for those who face the situation about which they wrote in their letters and to pray for all of us as we grow in valuing the gift of life.

- Loving and gracious God,

  We give you thanks and praise for the gift of this day and all the days that follow. Help us to see the value of the life you have given, not only to us but also to all your children. Send your Spirit of wisdom and courage to guide us in making decisions that hold sacred every moment we have. We pray for those who face difficult issues of life and death. Guide each of us with compassion to choose life always. We lift up for healing those who have suffered a loss; help them to realize that your love is ever present and that your generosity is unceasing. Amen.

Session Extensions

It's Wrong No Matter Who Does It (20 minutes)

Preparation

- Gather the following items:
  - ❏ copies of handout 13, "Reflection on Life Issues," one for each participant
  - ❏ pens or pencils

  1. Read the following story to the group:

  "That good-for-nothing finally got what he deserved!" Mr. Racjik shouted while pounding his fist on the breakfast table. "I wish they'd asked me to give the lethal injection—I'd have broken his stupid neck first." He noisily refolded the morning paper and tossed it onto an empty chair.

  "So one killing justifies another?" Mrs. Racjik challenged him. She was standing by the coffeemaker, waiting for the last drops to fall through the filter. "Do you know that the poor boy grew up in the slums of New York? He was beaten senseless whenever his mother's boyfriend got drunk—and even lost an eye when his cousin shot him during an argument."

  "So you're defending the murderer because he had a tough childhood?" Mr. Racjik said, the red rising in his cheeks. "What about the fact that he raped and murdered those cheerleaders? Do we just slap his hand because he couldn't control himself?"

  "What he did was wrong, I agree," Mrs. Racjik explained calmly, pouring herself a cup of coffee and sitting across from her husband. "But his execution hardly brings those girls back from the dead, does it? Now, there's just more blood spilt, and no one's better off! You're just like that crazy preacher in Florida who shot the doctor at the abortion clinic. By some twist of logic, he felt justified in killing the doctor to save the unborn."

"At least he was defending innocent babies," Mr. Racjik cried defensively. "That's why I vote for Republicans: they care about the unborn. You always vote for pro-abortion Democrats!"

"Well, there's more to politics than abortion!" Mrs. Racjik replied, beginning to lose her composure. She blew the steam from her coffee and sipped the hot liquid carefully before speaking again. "Anyway, I can understand why certain women seek an abortion. Beth Horner, my best friend in high school, had one because she was only fifteen, and her father threatened to kick her out of the house. And Samantha Sherwood terminated her last pregnancy because the fetus was deformed."

Shaking his head, Mr. Racjik reached for the loaf of bread in the center of the table, took two pieces, and dropped them into the toaster. "I guess I'd rather be against abortion and for the death penalty," he concluded, "than side with those who kill babies and coddle criminals."

Before Mrs. Racjik could say anything in response, her husband cleared his throat and nodded toward the door of the kitchen. Jill, their sixteen-year-old daughter, had just entered.

"Good morning, dear," her mother said sweetly. "I hope you slept well."

"Slept well? How could I sleep at all with the arguing going on out here?" she answered testily. "Come on! It's Saturday morning. People should be sleeping, not fighting."

"We were discussing, not fighting," Mr. Racjik corrected his daughter. "Besides, we don't need your permission to have a discussion."

"Maybe not, Dad," Jill said as she slipped into a chair by his side, "but the two of you need to think a little bit more before you have your next fight—I mean, discussion."

"Think? What do you mean, honey?" Mrs. Racjik was very curious to know what her daughter had in mind.

"Well, first, Dad says that killing murderers is okay but killing cheerleaders isn't. Then you say that killing murderers isn't okay but getting an abortion is. I just don't get it. If killing is wrong, it's wrong no matter who does it."

"How long were you standing outside the kitchen, Jill?" her father inquired. "Eavesdropping isn't polite, you know."

"I didn't have to eavesdrop. I could hear you in my bedroom," she huffed. "You two get so loud when you fight—I mean, discuss."

"She's right, Jim," Mrs. Racjik said. "It's no wonder she overheard us."

"Anyway, Mom and Dad," Jill said, covering a big yawn with her left hand, "I don't agree with either one of you. I think God loves all people, whether they're good or bad, and doesn't want anybody to be killed." She shook her head slightly. "Maybe you should pray today for a convict on death row, Dad, and Mom, you should pray for a pregnant teenager. I think everyone's life is worth at least a prayer or two, don't you?"

2. Distribute handout 13 to the participants, along with a pen or pencil. Allow 5 to 7 minutes for them to respond to the questions. Then invite the participants to share their responses with a partner.

3. Share with the participants the bullet points below, which are taken from pages 254–255 of the *CFH*:

• Sometimes the lives of others or even our own life may not be perfect, and life can make demands on us that are not what we want. Children and adults who are disabled or ill can require a great deal of demanding care. Sometimes other people can be annoying, inconvenient, or even our enemy. But each life is as precious to God as we are. We can never throw a life away. The beginning and end of every life is up to God, and only God.

• However, studies show that by the age of eighteen, the average child will see sixteen thousand murders on television! Sadly, so much exposure to killing, from cartoons to news programs, has the effect of making us less sensitive to the horror of taking another human life.

Ask the participants whether the parents in the story they heard demonstrate that they are able to maintain the "consistent approach to life" to which God and the Church call us.

4. Conduct a large group discussion based on the following questions:

• If a friend of yours became pregnant and did not know what to do, how would you respond?

• If a relative of yours were on death row, how would you act toward him or her?

5. Encourage the participants to get involved in appropriate efforts to end abortion and capital punishment. If time allows, brainstorm some first steps to take in getting involved.

(This activity is adapted from Lisa Calderone-Stewart and Ed Kunzman, *Straight from the Heart and Other Stories,* p. 36.)

Stories of Compassion (15 minutes)

1. Invite the participants to recall a time when they felt compassion toward another person. Ask them to describe the event by answering the following questions:

- How old were you?
- What moved you to compassion?
- How did this feel?

2. Share the story of Dorothy Day, as follows:

When Dorothy Day was a young child, at a time when many people couldn't find work, her father brought donuts home every Saturday morning. As she sat eating in her apartment in New York City, she could see ragged, hungry people walking the streets below. One day she suggested to her father that since he always brought a dozen donuts even though there were only three people in the family, perhaps she and her parents could eat just one and share the other nine with the people on the streets. Her father told her that this wasn't a good idea, but every Saturday morning for several weeks she brought it up again. Then one Saturday her father grew stern: "There's nothing we can do," he said. "Don't ever bring it up again." Dorothy refused to accept her father's analysis of things. She kept her compassion alive, spending time among poor people and finally opening the first Catholic Worker house of hospitality in 1933. Ever since that day, people influenced by Dorothy have been welcoming the homeless poor, offering a listening ear, a bowl of soup, and a bed to sleep in at night.

(adapted from Dorothy C. Bass and Don C. Richter, "Life," in *Way to Live Leader's Guide,* p. 14)

3. Ask the participants to reflect on the following questions:

- In the past week, when have you noticed someone experiencing compassion and offering assistance to others?
- Whom do you know personally whom you would describe as a person of compassion?

Ask the participants to think of an example of this person's compassion toward others and then to share their answer with a partner.

4. Conclude by inviting each participant to name one way he or she can be more compassionate toward others.

Promoting a Culture of Life (15 minutes)

Preparation

- Gather the following items:
  - ❏ copies of handout 14, "Promoting a Culture of Life," one for each participant
  - ❏ pens or pencils

1. Share the following with the participants:

- Pope John Paul II often talks about promoting a culture of life.
- Today we are going to look at a variety of human activities and ask the question, "Does this promote a culture of life or a culture of death?"
- Do you remember our definition of morality? "The goodness or evil of human acts" (*CCC*, no. 1749).
- What actions promote a culture of life: the good ones or the evil ones? What actions promote a culture of death?
- When the Pope talks about a culture of life, is he talking only about killing?
- God expects us to stand in awe of human life, to have profound respect for the dignity of the human person (*CFH*, p. 254).
- When you are working on the handout, try to decide whether the action in question shows "profound respect for the dignity of the human person."

2. Distribute copies of handout 14 and pens or pencils to the participants. Ask them to work with a partner. Allow 5 minutes for them to complete the handout.

3. Review their answers in the large group. Ask how telling a lie promotes death or why visiting a nursing home promotes life. Acknowledge that promoting life is more than just being "for" or "against" something. Promoting life means that all our actions, words, thoughts, and values work together to choose life.

Life in Abundance (10 minutes)

Preparation

- Gather the following items:
  - ❏ copies of the prayer on resource 3, "Abundance Prayer Card," one for each participant
  - ❏ a *Catholic Youth Bible* or other Bible, opened to John 10:10

TryThis
Building on the list provided in the article "Five Ways to Promote Life," on page 259 in *The Catholic Faith Handbook for Youth,* create a list of practical ways in which the participants can actively engage to promote life.

***Spirit & Song* connections**
- ◆ "Behind and Before Me," by Cyprian Consiglio
- ◆ "Lord of All Hopefulness," by Timothy R. Smith
- ◆ "Go Light Your World," by Chris Rice
- ◆ "Open My Eyes," by Jesse Manibusan

❑ a candle and matches

❑ a large basket filled with fresh fruit

❑ a tape player or a CD player

❑ a song with the theme of abundance

- Distribute one "Abundance Prayer Card" to each participant.
- Set up the prayer space with the Bible and the lit candle. Position the basket of fruit, and spread the prayer cards around the basket.

1. Begin the prayer with the sign of the cross.

2. Invite a participant to proclaim the Scripture passage from the Gospel of John 10:10. Then allow some time for quiet reflection.

3. Pose the following two questions:

- What does it mean to have abundant life?
- What would abundant life look like in our families, our high schools, our churches, and our world?

4. Say something like the following:

- The basket of fruit in our prayer space is one example of the abundance that God provides for us. We are fortunate to live in a place where food is plentiful. Jesus invites us to abundant life by following him. As we sing [name of selected song], I invite you to come forward and select a prayer card with the Scripture passage on it and to choose a piece of fruit to enjoy as a gift of God's abundance.

5. Conclude with the following prayer:

Shepherding God,
You lead us on the right path
And walk with us through the valleys.
Your goodness is our constant companion.
Be with us now and always as we journey through life.
Let our days and our deeds overflow with your love and your life.
Amen.

Options and Actions

- **Respect Life speaker.** Invite someone from the diocesan Respect Life office to speak to the group about the ways teens can show respect for all life.

- **Delve deeper.** Choose one of the many life issues raised up by the participants, and encourage them to investigate it further. What are the questions surrounding the particular issue? Where does the Church stand? How can we effect change with regard to this issue? What will be our first step?

- **Lifesavers.** Give each person a roll of LifeSavers™ candy and a slip of paper with the following two questions for reflection: How can I be a lifesaver to someone this week? How will I stand up for life this week? (Adapted from Maryann Hakowski, *Sharing the Sunday Scriptures with Youth: Cycle C,* p. 93)

- **Scandalized.** Share with the participants various newspaper reports of a recent scandal. Select a range of papers, from supermarket tabloids to fan magazines to responsible newspapers. Invite the participants to compare the different versions of the story by studying the kinds of words used, the style of grammar, and the overall tone of the stories. Ask which stories promote life and which spread scandal or promote death by their mood, tone, or word choice.

- **Respect for health.** Ask the participants to inventory what they do to promote their own health: for example, exercising, eating well, getting enough sleep, and refraining from ingesting excessive amounts of harmful substances (from sugar to drugs, alcohol, and tobacco). Then ask them to inventory the ways they compromise their health: for example, not doing any of the healthy things, wearing inappropriate clothing in winter, or engaging in unhealthy behavior such as binging and purging. Ask them to review the lists side by side. Overall, are they respecting their life more than they are damaging it? What can they do to respect their own life more?

Respecting Life

This session covers pages 253–264 of *The Catholic Faith Handbook for Youth*. For further exploration, check out paragraph numbers 2258–2330 of the *Catechism of the Catholic Church (CCC)*.

Session Summary

- The natural law God has put in our heart tells us that every human life has eternal value. From the unborn child to the person who has lived more than one hundred years, every life is sacred. Despite the most advanced scientific discoveries and technologies, the mystery of life and death ultimately leads us to God.

- God expects us to stand in awe of human life, to have profound respect for the dignity of the human person. The word *respect* means "to look again." But no generation before has had to consider so many complex and controversial issues that threaten the dignity of life.

- We are made in the image of God—each and every one of us. No exceptions. From the first chapter of Genesis to the most recent edition of the *Catechism,* this statement about who we are and what kind of person God wants us to be is at the heart of morality. It is the foundation for loving other people, our God, and ourselves.

- Sometimes the lives of others or even our own life may not be perfect, and life can make demands on us that are not what we want. Children and adults who are disabled or ill can require a great deal of demanding care. Sometimes other people can be annoying, inconvenient, or even our enemy. But each life is as precious to God as we are. We can never throw a life away. The beginning and end of every life is up to God, and only God.

- However, studies show that by the age of eighteen, the average child will see sixteen thousand murders on television! Sadly, so much exposure to killing, from cartoons to news programs, has the effect of making us less sensitive to the horror of taking another human life.

- Although murder is clearly wrong, what about killing in self-defense? The Church teaches that we have the right to stop someone from inflicting harm on us or others. But if possible we must avoid taking the life of the one who threatens us.

- The issue of the death penalty presents a major challenge to society. The majority of the people in the United States support the use of the death penalty, also called capital punishment. Today the Church teaches that capital punishment is moral only when it is impossible to effectively defend human life in any other way. Because we have prison systems that can adequately protect society, Pope John Paul II has said that moral reasons for using the death penalty "are very rare, if not practically non-existent"[1] (*CCC*, number 2267). The Church recognizes that even the worst immoral act does not take away a person's God-given dignity.

- War, as an act of self-defense, is another challenging issue when we talk about respect for human life. Although armed conflict can be a valid way of protecting against unjust aggressors, we know that war brings evils and injustices to all of society.
- So the Church teaches that all citizens and all governments must do everything they can to avoid war.
- The reality is that war still happens, and countries must defend themselves. The principles of legitimate self-defense are just as applicable for nations as they are for individuals. However, war must be a last resort, and over the centuries the Church developed criteria that must be met if a war is morally permissible.
- One of the most controversial life issues in society today is abortion. Abortion intentionally stops the development of an unborn child. It is controversial because not everyone agrees with the Church that from conception, a child has the right to life.
- Recent scientific and technological breakthroughs show that signs of life are present long before a mother and father are aware that they have conceived a child. Science can use this information to promote respect for life, or in ways that are not so respectful. There are serious moral questions about genetic engineering, cloning, and other ways of conceiving life in ways that God did not intend.
- Moral issues exist on the other end of human life. One of those issues is euthanasia, also called mercy killing. Proponents of euthanasia make it an issue of human freedom, saying that people—or their family if the person is incapable of making their own decisions—have a right to choose to end their life. But the Church teaches that euthanasia is a serious moral wrong. The Church considers the act of intentionally causing the death of a human being to be murder, regardless of the motive or the circumstances.
- Suicide is also a grave offense against the fifth commandment. As sacred as life is, it can certainly seem overwhelming at times. But suicide, the taking of your own life, goes against human nature. As human beings, created by God, we are meant to preserve our own life as well as the lives of others. Suicide is the ultimate rejection of love of self, love of God, and love of neighbor.
- Respect for life also includes caring for the spiritual life of other people. Scandal is an attitude or behavior that deliberately leads another person to sin, causing harm to their spiritual life. Things we do, say, or wear can

be scandalous. For example, offering alcohol to someone who is underage is scandalous behavior.

- The fifth commandment, "You shall not kill," also covers respect for health as part of respect for life. We are wonderfully made—body, mind, and soul. When any aspect of our being is hurting, we cannot be whole, the way God made us. As individuals we must have respect for our own health, avoiding all kinds of excess: the abuse of food, alcohol, tobacco, or drugs.

1. John Paul II, *Evangelium vitae* 56.

(The summary point labeled *CCC* is from the *Catechism of the Catholic Church* for use in the United States of America, page number 2267. Copyright © 1994 by the United States Catholic Conference, Inc.—Libreria Editrice Vaticana. Used with permission.)

(All summary points are taken from *The Catholic Faith Handbook for Youth,* by Brian Singer-Towns et al. [Winona, MN: Saint Mary's Press, 2004], pages 253–262. Copyright © 2004 by Saint Mary's Press. All rights reserved.)

Talk Points

- Talk about five things that make life worth living.
- Talk about current songs or movies that promote life as important and valuable.
- What factors are necessary to promote and ensure a society that embraces a culture of life?
- Research the case of someone who is about to be executed or who has recently been executed. Find at least four media reports about the case, preferably from different sources.

Abundance Prayer Card

Directions: Copy the verse and the image on thick paper stock, and cut along the dotted lines. Laminate the cards if possible.

I came that they may have
LIFE,
and have it
ABUNDANTLY!

(John 10:10, NRSV)

I came that they may have
LIFE,
and have it
ABUNDANTLY!

(John 10:10, NRSV)

I came that they may have
LIFE,
and have it
ABUNDANTLY!

(John 10:10, NRSV)

I came that they may have
LIFE,
and have it
ABUNDANTLY!

(John 10:10, NRSV)

Overview

Because sexuality is such an important issue in the life of contemporary adolescents, two sessions (chapters 7 and 8) cover the many elements of this topic. This first session explores the positive nature of sexuality and its relationship to God. This session includes the topics of marriage and chastity; it also explores the sixth commandment (fidelity to sexual relations within a sacramental marriage) and the foundational principle of the ninth commandment (purity of heart).

Outcomes

◆ The learner will appreciate God's gift of sexuality.
◆ The learner will understand that marriage is the appropriate place for the full expression of the gift of sexuality.
◆ The learner will explore the value of chastity in marriage and in the single life.
◆ The learner will understand the reasons for the exclusive expression of sexual relations in a sacramental marriage, revealed in the sixth commandment, and the value of purity of heart, which is the basis of the ninth commandment.

Background Reading

◆ This session covers some elements of pages 265–275 of *The Catholic Faith Handbook for Youth (CFH)*. Chapter 8 covers other topics from these pages.
◆ For further exploration, check out paragraph numbers 2331–2350, 2360–2375, 2392–2395, 2397–2398, 2517–2524, 2527, and 2531–2533 of the *Catechism*.

◆ Scriptural connections: Gen. 1:26–27 (God made man and woman in his image.), John 15:12 (Love one another.), 1 Cor. 6:17–20 (the body as a temple)

◆ *Catholic Youth Bible* article connections: "A Very Special Gift" (Lev. 18:1–30), "Living Well" (1 Cor. 6:12–20), "True Love Waits" (1 Thess. 4:1–8)

Core Session

Three Legs of the Stool (45 minutes)

Preparation

- Gather the following items:
  - ❏ copies of handout 15, "Respecting Sexuality: The Gift of Sexuality," one for each participant
  - ❏ paper
  - ❏ scissors
  - ❏ markers, pens, or pencils
  - ❏ masking tape
  - ❏ acorns, walnuts, or another kind of nut that will roll, one for every two participants
  - ❏ newsprint
- Review the summary points in step 4 of this session and the relevant material on pages 265–275 of *The Catholic Faith Handbook for Youth (CFH)*. Be prepared to share the information with the young people.
- Prepare for the first part of the activity by cutting large circles, one for every two participants, from some of the sheets of paper.

  1. Begin by asking the participants to find a partner to work with. Give each pair a paper circle that you cut out ahead of time, three sheets of plain paper, and one acorn or other nut. Instruct them to prepare the three sheets of paper separately by printing one phrase on each sheet: "For Life," "For Love," and "For Pleasure," respectively. On the circle they should print the phrase "Integrated Sexual Relationship." Instruct them to roll the sheets of paper lengthwise into three tubes about 1½ inches in diameter and to secure the paper tubes with tape.

  2. Invite the participants to spend about 5 minutes trying to accomplish the following task:

TryThis

If time allows, consider having the participants return to the partner with whom they made the stool, and invite them to rewrite one of the media examples to reflect Church teaching in the message. As a primer, ask this question: "What would these songs, movies, or television shows look like if they were conveying the message that sexual relations belong within a loving, sacramental marriage?" Allow the participants to share how they rewrote the examples.

- Using only the paper circle, the paper tubes, and the tape, your challenge is to make a stool that is sturdy enough to hold the acorn on it.
- I'd like you to start by trying to do it with only two tubes.
- After you've tried with two tubes, whether you succeed or fail, try it with all three tubes.

3. When all have completed the task, ask them what they learned about making a stool that will stand up. Invite them to think for a moment about the words on the "seat" and on the "legs" of the stool. Invite them to figure out the purpose of this exercise.

4. Conduct a brief presentation on the theme of Catholic teaching on sexuality, using key phrases from the preceding activity and the bullet points below, which are taken from pages 265–273 of the *CFH:*

- Most of the time, when we refer to the word *sex,* we think of our body, even though sexual acts also involve our mind, our emotions, and even our spirituality.
- The trouble is, many people try to take sex out of the larger picture, making the gift much less than it was intended to be. It would be like taking a fine piece of art and using it for scrap paper. It will work, but you destroy the beauty and the real purpose of the masterpiece.
- The Church's teaching on sex and sexuality is like all her moral teachings. It is based on human reason, on the Scriptures, and on Tradition. Although some people think that the Church has nothing positive to say about the topic, the opposite is true. Both the Scriptures and Tradition begin with the basic teaching that sexuality is one of God's greatest and most beautiful gifts to us.
- The sixth (You shall not commit adultery.) and ninth (You shall not covet your neighbor's wife.) commandments simply remind us that the misuse of such a great gift can cause great harm.
- Understanding our intimate relationships with others begins with understanding our own sexuality. God did not intend for our sexuality to be separate from our heart, our mind, and our spirit.
- Sexual activity, the physical expression of our sexuality, enables us to relate to another human being in a way that says, "This relationship is special." Sexual expression should be a sign of our commitment to the other person. Simple kissing, or even holding hands, says that we are more than just friends. Sexual expression that involves genital activity is reserved for real, permanent love relationships. Real sex belongs within a real love relationship that will stand the test of time. It belongs in sacramental marriage.
- Why does the Church make such a big deal out of sex belonging only in marriage? To answer that question, we need to look at how God made the act of sexual intercourse different for humans than for any other species. Simply stated, God made sex for three purposes:

- ○ Sex creates new life.
  - ○ Sex expresses loving union.
  - ○ Sex brings us joy and pleasure.

  It is important to keep all three purposes in mind, because they cannot be separated from one another; they are integrated—parts of the whole picture. If only one or two of these is present, God's plan is derailed.
- Dating is a temporary arrangement—a testing ground for relationships. Even being engaged is not quite permanent. Thus neither a dating relationship nor being engaged provides the commitment necessary for sexual intercourse. But Christian marriage does. It is the only relationship that ensures that all three aspects of sex are integrated, woven into the minds, bodies, and spiritualities of the couple.
- Marriage is a covenant, a sacred promise that people freely make and intend to keep faithfully. Sex is the sign of that covenant, that communion.
- Integrity requires honesty and authenticity in what you say and what you do. Sexual integrity is about being honest with yourself and others about how committed you are to a relationship. Rationalizing or leading people on for the purpose of sexual pleasure is deceptive. The Church's term for sexual integrity is chastity.
- Christ is the model for chastity, a virtue that requires integration of our sexuality with the whole person—body, mind, and spirit. Every person, single or married, is called to be chaste, to be healthy and honest, and to respect the sexuality of self and others.
- But practicing sexual integrity and chastity is easier if we develop attitudes that not only form our conscience the right way but also help us to live according to what we know is right. The sixth beatitude, "Blessed are the pure of heart, for they shall see God," is Jesus' message that fulfills the sixth and ninth commandments.

5. Remind the participants of what they saw happen to the paper stool when they used only two legs. Suggest that the next step is to take a look at what happens in a sexual relationship when one or more elements of a *whole* relationship are missing.

6. Ask the participants to share what they might believe about sexuality and sexuality activity if their only source of information was the popular media (television, movies, music). Have them share not only what they would learn but also which media portrayed it. Write down their responses on newsprint.

7. Next ask for volunteers to point out the examples just written on newsprint that conflict with the Church's teachings on sexuality.

Familyconnections

◆ Consider conducting a session for parents that offers information on how they can support the healthy sexual growth of their son or daughter.

◆ Suggest that the participants and their parents develop a list of ways, other than in sexual relations, for people to say "I love you." This activity can provide young people with a number of alternatives for expressing affection for another person without having sex.

◆ Suggest that the participants talk to a married couple (parents, grandparents, or friends). Provide the participants with questions to ask the couple. They should first ask the couple whether they are willing to talk about their relationship before they got married and now. If they are willing, the participants can ask:

◇ When you were dating, did you talk about whether you'd like to have children or about other ways that your relationship could be life-giving for others?

◇ At what point in your relationship did you feel certain that you wanted to raise a family together?

8. Review for the participants the key points of Church teaching that you shared in step 4 of this activity.

9. Close by inviting the participants to consider what they hope for in the three purposes of a sexual relationship and also what they hope to find in the person they will eventually be called to join in sacramental marriage. Be sure to note that the content of this session was drawn from chapter 27 of the *CFH*. Encourage the participants to read and review it in the next few days.

Session Extensions

Chastity Is a Choice (15 minutes)

Preparation
• Gather the following items:
  ❑ colored 4 x 6-inch index cards, cut in half, enough for two or three cards per participant
  ❑ fine-tip markers or gel pens of various colors

1. Introduce the concept of chastity by using the following bullet points, which are taken from pages 270–274 of the *CFH:*
• We have talked quite a bit about the integration of sexuality with our body, mind, and spirit.
• Integrity requires honesty and authenticity in what you say and what you do. Sexual integrity is about being honest with yourself and others about how committed you are to a relationship. Rationalizing or leading people on for the purpose of sexual pleasure is deceptive. The Church's term for sexual integrity is chastity.
• Christ is the model for chastity, a virtue that requires integration of our sexuality with the whole person—body, mind, and spirit. Every person, single or married, is called to be chaste, to be healthy and honest, and to respect the sexuality of self and others.
• Chastity does take practice. Your body is telling you that sex feels good, and hundreds of cultural messages a day tell you it is okay to act on your sexual instincts. Some adults will bluntly state that teenagers are going to do it anyway. What those voices are suggesting is that young people don't have the discipline to practice sexual integrity, to be chaste.
• The Church has more hope and higher expectations for you.
• But practicing sexual integrity and chastity is easier if we develop attitudes that not only form our conscience the right way but also help us to live according to what we know is right. The sixth beatitude, "Blessed are the pure of heart, for they shall see God," is Jesus' message that fulfills the sixth and ninth commandments.

- What does it mean to be pure of heart? The *Catechism* refers to the heart as the seat of moral personality. Forming our conscience is the work of the head, but our heart "enables us to see *according* to God. . . . [Purity of heart] lets us perceive the human body—ours and our neighbor's—as a temple of the Holy Spirit, a manifestation of divine beauty" (*CCC,* no. 2519).

- Rather than seeing chastity as a burden, consider the freedom that it gives: freedom from worry about pregnancy, disease, and emotional wounds that lead to the scar tissue of vulnerability. Sexual integrity is the freedom to be healthy and whole—according to God's design.

2. Divide the participants into small groups of four or five. Distribute the index cards and pens to each small group. Instruct the participants to come up with slogans or encouraging statements about what chastity means to them: What are their ideas on the meaning of chastity? How does a person live the virtue of chastity today? Have the participants refer to the section in the *CFH* that addresses chastity (pages 270–272) as a resource for this activity.

3. Have the young people share their cards with one another. Brainstorm ways they might use these cards, such as developing a poster to promote chastity, creating an insert for the parish bulletin or Web site, using them as a prayer focus each day, carrying one in a wallet or purse, and so forth.

Presenting and Respecting the Whole Person (20 minutes)

Preparation
- Gather the following items:
  - ❏ pens or pencils
  - ❏ paper

1. Invite the participants to reflect individually on what they believe is their most attractive quality. Assure them that you will not ask them to share their answers to this question.

2. Then ask the following reflection questions:
- What is your most attractive quality?
- Why do you believe this is the most attractive thing about you?
- Has anyone ever affirmed that this quality is an attractive part of who you are?
- How would you feel if this quality were the only thing people saw as attractive about you?

◇ What are some things in your relationship that give you real joy?
◇ Did you think about what love would mean during the hard times?
◇ Where does God fit in your relationship?
◇ Has your understanding of love changed over the years?
◇ What advice would you give an engaged couple who are approaching the wedding date?

Try This
Using the article "Ten Ways to Practice Chastity," on page 270 of *The Catholic Faith Handbook for Youth,* conduct a discussion on how these ideas are useful for living a life of sexual integrity. Then invite the participants to add to the list.

JournalACTIVITIES

◆ What characteristics do you think make up a whole, integrated human person made by God and in loving relationship with God? Which of these characteristics have you already developed? Which could you develop more fully? Write down some steps you can take this week to make yourself more whole and integrated.

◆ Other than what you've read in *The Catholic Faith Handbook for Youth (CFH)* or learned in this session, what reasons can you think of for abstaining from sex until you are called to join a spouse in Catholic sacramental marriage? (*CFH*, p. 275)

◆ Write a prayer to ask God for the values and the strength to be a sexually healthy, whole, and holy person.

• How would you feel if this quality were the only part of you that people valued?

3. Invite the participants to share their responses only to the last two questions. Direct them not to share what they believe is their most attractive aspect, but only their answers to the two questions.

4. Conduct a brief presentation using the bullet points below, which are taken from pages 266–274 of *The Catholic Faith Handbook for Youth:*

• The Scriptures tell us that not only are we made in God's image, God intentionally created us male and female.

• We can't remove our sexuality from who we are, any more than we can separate our brain from our body or our spirit from our mind.

• Every person, single or married, is called to be chaste, to be healthy and honest, and to respect the sexuality of self and others.

• The ninth commandment, "You shall not covet your neighbor's wife," is closely related to the sixth commandment against adultery. It speaks of lust and carnal concupiscence.

• The gift the Holy Spirit gives us to keep our desires in check is the virtue of temperance. Temperance is about using our will to overcome our instincts.

• The virtue of modesty protects our intimate center. We don't tell just anybody our most private secrets; we should not let just anybody see or touch our sacred places.

• The clothes you wear can send unintended messages, and outfits that leave little to the imagination may reveal more than you want. It is wrong to try to intentionally cause sexual excitement in another person.

• But respect goes both ways. It is never right to take advantage of someone sexually, regardless of his or her dress or behavior.

5. As a group, discuss what these Church teachings reveal to us about valuing others and ourselves as whole persons. What is the result of seeing someone as only an object for our enjoyment? Why is it important to represent ourselves as whole persons? What message do we send when we allow ourselves, by the way we dress or act, to be seen merely as an object?

6. Ask the participants to reflect on the following questions and to record their answers privately on the sheet of paper.

• What are a few examples of times (think about movies, television, and advertisements) when I have viewed an individual as an object?

• Have there been times when I represented myself as less than a whole person because of my actions or my clothing?

• What is one thing I can do to help me not view other people as objects or possessions?

- How can I better represent myself as a whole person: body, mind, and spirit?

7. Challenge the participants to be aware of the manner in which they look at others and present themselves.

Body Meditation (15 minutes)

Preparation

- Set up a comfortable space with dimmed lighting, reflective music playing in the background, and a lit candle.

Ask the young people to find a comfortable space on the floor where they will be able to close their eyes and relax. Wait until everyone is settled and ready to begin. Introduce the guided meditation as an opportunity to get in touch with Jesus. Ask them to listen to your voice as you lead them through this reflection. [*Note:* Read in a soft, gentle voice, making sure they can hear you above the reflective music. To allow the young people to reflect, pause briefly whenever you see an ellipsis (. . .).]

- Close your eyes . . . listen to the rhythm of your breathing . . . slowly . . . in . . . out . . . relaxing your body . . . letting go of all of today's concerns . . . clearing your mind. . . .

    Imagine yourself in the beginning of time . . . God is creating the sky . . . the moon and the stars . . . the planets and the earth . . . the flowers and the animals . . . and the sea. . . . Look around at the beauty being created. . . . Now notice God creating man . . . and woman . . . and God declares all creation beautiful and good. . . .

    Breathe in, and experience God breathing life into creation . . . a creation that has been made in God's own image. . . .

    Picture your body . . . a body that reflects the artwork of a loving God. . . . Notice how unique and beautiful you are . . . the color of your eyes and hair . . . the tone and feel of your skin . . . the features of your face, your hands, your feet. . . . Feel your body resting in the open hands of God . . . a body that is still being formed and developed . . . a body that is unique in all the world. . . .

    With full awareness of your body, its beauty, its uniqueness, you notice a man walking toward you. . . . You feel calm and at peace as he comes closer. . . . You notice his face and look deeply into his eyes . . . the eyes of Jesus. . . .

VARIATION:
Large Group
Bring in magazine advertisements that focus on showing only one part of a person. Countless ads show only an individual's leg, chest, hand, or torso. Ask these questions: What message does this convey? Is one part of this person more valuable than the whole person?

Spirit & Song connections

- "My Life Is in Your Hands," by Kathy Troccoli and Bill Montvilo
- "Strength for the Journey," by Michael John Poirier
- "I Will Lift Up My Eyes," by Cyprian Consiglio

You see how comfortable Jesus is about his body . . . his sexuality . . . gifts he received when he became one of us. . . . His firm but gentle hands reach out to embrace you, and as he gathers you into his arms, you feel his warmth and power. . . .

You look at Jesus and begin to share your concerns with him about your own sexuality . . . your fears . . . your worries . . . your hopes. . . .

When you finish speaking, Jesus looks deep within you, and you know that he has heard you and your concerns. . . . As he gazes at you, he begins to speak, to respond to what you have just told him. . . . Listen to his response now. . . .

Jesus finishes speaking to you and reaches to embrace you one last time before he leaves. . . . As he turns away, you experience the warmth of the sun upon your face . . . and you feel wholeness inside. . . .

You begin to walk toward the present. . . . Slowly you become aware of the room you are now in. . . . You sense the other people around you. . . . You are ready to return to your life renewed . . . refreshed . . . and at peace. . . .

When you are ready . . . slowly open your eyes . . . and sit quietly until you are fully aware of your surroundings.

Slowly turn the lights up and the music off as the young people conclude their meditation.

(Michael Theisen, *Sexuality: Challenges and Choices,* p. 49)

TryThis
The article "True Love Waits," on page 271 of *The Catholic Faith Handbook for Youth* is a great prayer alternative.

LiVE it!

Options and Actions

• **Open our eyes.** Challenge the youth to keep track of any images they come in contact with over the next week that portray disrespect for the gifts of sexuality and relationships. Ask them also to keep track of images that present sexuality and relationships in line with Church teaching. Next time you gather, take a few moments to share how easy or difficult it was finding positive images as compared to locating unhealthy images.

- **"True love waits"** is an international campaign that challenges teenagers to remain sexually abstinent until marriage. The National Federation for Catholic Youth Ministry (NFCYM) offers a program resource packet at *www.nfcym.org.*

- **Treasure sexuality.** Invite the participants, alone or in groups, to write the word *treasure* down the left side of a sheet of paper. Ask them to think of ways they can live a life of sexual integrity. They should do this by using each letter in the verb *treasure* as their starting point (adapted from Nora Bradbury-Haehl, *Scripture Walk Senior High: Discipleship,* p. 74).

- **What could you say?** Given all that you have read in *The Catholic Faith Handbook for Youth* or learned in this session about the beauty, integrity, and purpose of sexuality, why would someone choose to be sexually active before they're ready for marriage? What could you say to convince him or her to wait? (*CFH,* p. 275)

Mediaconnections

- Check out Web sites that promote chastity and abstinence, such as *www.respectincorporated.com* and *www.friendsfirst.org.*

- Watch a movie with a love-relationship theme. Is God visible in the love depicted?

- Watch an episode of one of the reality television programs that involve bachelors, bachelorettes, fiancés, marriages, or testing relationships. Try to maintain your role as observer and not get hooked into the story line. Make a list of all the issues the performers talk about as being important to them in a relationship, and count how many times they refer to each issue. When the program is over, count how many times the performers talked about pleasure issues as being important, how many times they talked about life issues, and how many times they talked about love issues. Are these people headed toward balanced relationships?

Respecting Sexuality: The Gift of Sexuality

This session covers some elements of pages 265–275 of *The Catholic Faith Handbook for Youth*. Chapter 8 covers other topics from these pages. For further exploration, check out paragraph numbers 2331–2350, 2360–2375, 2392–2395, 2397–2398, 2517–2524, 2527, and 2531–2533 of the *Catechism of the Catholic Church (CCC)*.

Session Summary

- Most of the time, when we refer to the word *sex,* we think of our body, even though sexual acts also involve our mind, our emotions, and even our spirituality.
- The trouble is, many people try to take sex out of the larger picture, making the gift much less than it was intended to be. It would be like taking a fine piece of art and using it for scrap paper. It will work, but you destroy the beauty and the real purpose of the masterpiece.
- The Church's teaching on sex and sexuality is like all her moral teachings. It is based on human reason, on the Scriptures, and on Tradition. Although some people think that the Church has nothing positive to say about the topic, the opposite is true. Both the Scriptures and Tradition begin with the basic teaching that sexuality is one of God's greatest and most beautiful gifts to us.
- The sixth (You shall not commit adultery.) and ninth (You shall not covet your neighbor's wife.) commandments simply remind us that the misuse of such a great gift can cause great harm.
- Understanding our intimate relationships with others begins with understanding our own sexuality. God did not intend for our sexuality to be separate from our heart, our mind, and our spirit.
- Sexual activity, the physical expression of our sexuality, enables us to relate to another human being in a way that says, "This relationship is special." Sexual expression should be a sign of our commitment to the other person. Simple kissing, or even holding hands, says that we are more than just friends. Sexual expression that involves genital activity is reserved for real, permanent love relationships. Real sex belongs within a real love relationship that will stand the test of time. It belongs in sacramental marriage.

- Why does the Church make such a big deal out of sex belonging only in marriage? To answer that question, we need to look at how God made the act of sexual intercourse different for humans than for any other species. Simply stated, God made sex for three purposes:
  ○ Sex creates new life.
  ○ Sex expresses loving union.
  ○ Sex brings us joy and pleasure.
  It is important to keep all three purposes in mind, because they cannot be separated from one another; they are integrated—parts of the whole picture. If only one or two of these is present, God's plan is derailed.
- Dating is a temporary arrangement—a testing ground for relationships. Even being engaged is not quite permanent. Thus neither a dating relationship nor being engaged provides the commitment necessary for sexual intercourse. But Christian marriage does. It is the only relationship that ensures that all three aspects of sex are integrated, woven into the minds, bodies, and spiritualities of the couple.
- Marriage is a covenant, a sacred promise that people freely make and intend to keep faithfully. Sex is the sign of that covenant, that communion.
- We have talked quite a bit about the integration of sexuality with our body, mind, and spirit.
- Integrity requires honesty and authenticity in what you say and what you do. Sexual integrity is about being honest with yourself and others about how committed you are to a relationship. Rationalizing or leading people on for the purpose of sexual pleasure is deceptive. The Church's term for sexual integrity is chastity.
- Christ is the model for chastity, a virtue that requires integration of our sexuality with the whole person—body, mind, and spirit. Every person, single or married, is called to be chaste, to be healthy and honest, and to respect the sexuality of self and others.
- Chastity does take practice. Your body is telling you that sex feels good, and hundreds of cultural messages a day tell you it is okay to act on your sexual instincts. Some adults will bluntly state that teenagers are going to do it anyway. What those voices are suggesting is that young people don't have the discipline to practice sexual integrity, to be chaste.
- The Church has more hope and higher expectations for you.
- But practicing sexual integrity and chastity is easier if we develop attitudes that not only form our conscience the right way but also help us to live according to what we know is right. The sixth beatitude, "Blessed are the pure of heart, for they shall see God," is Jesus' message that fulfills the sixth and ninth commandments.

- What does it mean to be pure of heart? The *Catechism* refers to the heart as the seat of moral personality. Forming our conscience is the work of the head, but our heart "enables us to see *according* to God. [Purity of heart] lets us perceive the human body—ours and our neighbor's—as a temple of the Holy Spirit, a manifestation of divine beauty" (*CCC,* number 2519).
- Rather than seeing chastity as a burden, consider the freedom that it gives: freedom from worry about pregnancy, disease, and emotional wounds that lead to the scar tissue of vulnerability. Sexual integrity is the freedom to be healthy and whole—according to God's design.
- The virtue of modesty protects our intimate center. We don't tell just anybody our most private secrets; we should not let just anybody see or touch our sacred places.
- The clothes you wear can send unintended messages, and outfits that leave little to the imagination may reveal more than you want. It is wrong to intentionally try to cause sexual excitement in another person.
- But respect goes both ways. It is never right to take advantage of someone sexually, regardless of his or her dress or behavior.

(The summary point labeled *CCC* is from the *Catechism of the Catholic Church* for use in the United States of America, number 2519. Copyright © 1994 by the United States Catholic Conference, Inc.—Libreria Editrice Vaticana. Used with permission.)

(All summary points are taken from *The Catholic Faith Handbook for Youth,* by Brian Singer-Towns et al. [Winona, MN: Saint Mary's Press, 2004], pages 265–275. Copyright © 2004 by Saint Mary's Press. All rights reserved.)

Talk Points

- Talk with a friend about the characteristics that most clearly define you as a male or a female. What impact do these traits have on your relationship with others?
- Where have you gotten your attitudes and values regarding sex and sexuality?
- What positive qualities characterize the whole person that is you? How can you nurture and grow these qualities so they will be even more of a gift to the person you eventually marry?

8

Respecting Sexuality:
The Challenge of Sexuality

AT A GLANCE

Study It

Core Session

◆ Completely in God's Love
(45 minutes)

Session Extensions

◆ All Are Welcome at the
Table
(20 minutes)
◆ Temptation Around Every
Corner
(20 minutes)

Pray It

◆ Compassionate Love
(10 minutes)

Live It

◆ Attitudes toward sexuality
◆ Top ten
◆ How would you feel?
◆ Not two but one

Overview

Because sexuality is such an important issue in the life of contemporary adolescents, two sessions (chapters 7 and 8) cover the many elements of this topic. This second session explores the sexual challenges that young people confront in our time and culture, and it encourages them to face these challenges in the context of the sacred gift of sexuality that God has given them. This session focuses on the sixth and ninth commandments, which address the sexual temptations present in our society.

Outcomes

◆ The learner will understand how sexual sin separates us from God's plan and how chastity strengthens our relationship with God.
◆ The learner will confront the sexual temptations of today's culture, which affect both single and married people.
◆ The learner will understand the situation of the homosexual person in the context of God's gift of sexuality.

Background Reading

◆ This session covers some elements of pages 265–275 of *The Catholic Faith Handbook for Youth*. Chapter 7 covers other topics from these pages.
◆ For further exploration, check out paragraph numbers 2351–2359, 2376–2391, 2396, 2399–2400, 2514–2516, 2525–2526, and 2528–2530 of the *Catechism.*
◆ Scriptural connections: 2 Sam. 11:1–17 (David commits adultery with Bathsheba, then tries to cover it up.), Rom. 1:18–32 (the guilt of humankind)

◆ *Catholic Youth Bible* article connections: "Lust and Its Consequences" (2 Sam. 11:1–5), "The Illusion of Pornography" (Song 2:1–17), "Homo- sexuality and AIDS" (Rom. 1:18–32)

Core Session

Completely in God's Love (45 minutes)

Preparation

- Gather the following items:
  - ❏ copies of handout 16, "Respecting Sexuality: The Challenge of Sexuality," one for each participant
  - ❏ one sheet of newsprint for the presenter
  - ❏ a marker
  - ❏ four pieces of wide masking tape, approximately 8 to 10 inches in length
- Review the summary points in step 3 of this session and the relevant material on pages 265–275 of *The Catholic Faith Handbook for Youth (CFH)*. Be prepared to share the information with the young people.
- In addressing this challenging and important topic, be prepared for difficult questions. Don't hesitate to admit to the participants that you don't know an answer, but assure them that you will find out for them. Be sure to follow up with the correct answer.

    1. Begin the session by drawing a large circle on a sheet of newsprint. Inside the circle draw a figure of a teenager. The drawing need not be perfect, but it has to be large, though not extending outside the circle at any point. Tell the group that the circle you have drawn serves as a visual representation of God's love.

    2. As you discuss the topics of lust, fornication, masturbation, and pornography in the presentation in step 3, write each of these terms in sequence on a separate piece of masking tape. Place each tape segment somewhere on the newsprint drawing of the teenager. Three restrictions apply in placing the tape:

- A major portion of the tape segment must cover part of the teenager's figure.
- Do not stack one tape segment directly on top of another.

- Turn over a small corner of the tape so that you can remove the entire tape segment from the drawing if need be.

   3. Conduct a presentation on chastity, using the bullet points below, which are taken from pages 266–272 of the *CFH:*

- Both the Scriptures and Tradition begin with the basic teaching that sexuality is one of God's greatest and most beautiful gifts to us.
- The sixth (You shall not commit adultery.) and ninth (You shall not covet your neighbor's wife.) commandments simply remind us that the misuse of such a great gift can cause great harm.
- Why does the Church make such a big deal out of sex belonging only in marriage? To answer that question, we need to look at how God made the act of sexual intercourse different for humans than for any other species. Simply stated, God made sex for three purposes:
  ○ Sex creates new life.
  ○ Sex expresses loving union.
  ○ Sex brings us joy and pleasure.
- If sex was *only* about experiencing pleasure, we would be more like animals than humans. People who have sex just because it feels good are missing the point. They are acting on instinct—body only, no heart or head involved.
- The ninth commandment, "You shall not covet your neighbor's wife," is closely related to the sixth commandment against adultery. It speaks of lust and carnal concupiscence. These intimidating words simply mean that the life forces within us have a dark side. Men often experience this dark side as an overwhelming desire for sexual pleasure. Women often experience it as a need to have sex in order to hold on to a relationship.
- The gift the Holy Spirit gives us to keep our desires in check is the virtue called temperance. Temperance is about using our will to overcome our instincts.
- The demons of the dark side will always be present, threatening our good intentions. Fornication is a biblical term that refers to sex outside of marriage. Television shows may influence you to think that casual sex is a sign of the times, and that everybody is doing it, but the reality is that more and more teenagers are questioning the wisdom of sex without permanent commitment. Recent studies show that the majority of adolescents who have had sex, said they wish they had waited.
- Masturbation, genital activity alone or with another person that does not result in sexual intercourse, is also a sin against chastity. It is all about pleasure without regard for life or real love. Sins against chastity include other forms of genital sexual activity that stop short of sexual intercourse, such as petting or oral sex. They are forms of exploitation, and are not appropriate sexual expressions for semicommitted love.

Journal ACTIVITIES

- ◆ What are the characteristics that most clearly define you as a male or as a female? What impact do these traits have on your relationship with others? Try to come up with a specific example.
- ◆ How does pornography—whether it is considered soft porn, like in movies, or hard-core porn, as in some magazines or on the Internet—exploit and cheapen the gift of sexuality? (*CFH*, p. 275)
- ◆ The earth, air, water, and the rest of the natural environment are gifts from God. Our sexuality is a gift from God. Make a list of the parallels between caring for the environment and caring for your sexual purity. Make a list of the differences. How can your commitment to the environment spur you on to care more for yourself?

- One of the most common offenses against the sixth and ninth commandments is pornography. The Internet has made this evil more accessible to young people. Pornography is dangerous because it violates human dignity. It takes the gift of sexuality and makes it an object to be exploited and abused.

4. Invite the participants to express any questions they have at this point. You might get challenging questions about masturbation, premarital sex, and pornography. Help the participants answer their own questions by referring to the sixth and ninth commandments.

5. After the question period, ask the participants to look at the newsprint drawing with tape on it. Ask the following questions, and share these responses from the *CFH* with the group:

- What does the circle symbolize?
- God is love (*CFH*, p. 46).
- God loves us more than we could possibly imagine (*CFH*, p. 46).
- Using the visual images of the young person in the center of the circle and of God's love as represented by the entire circle, how do you consider that the sins of lust, fornication, masturbation, and pornography separate us or hide us from God's love?

In the discussion, refer to the bullet points below, which are taken from pages 212–214 of the *CFH:*

- When we choose to do wrong instead of doing good, we commit sin, and we hurt our relationship with our self, with others, and with God.
- When we sin, we reject God's will for us to be good.
- A mortal sin is a serious offense against God.
- The Ten Commandments specify the issues that constitute grave matter.
- Christian morality, then, is being the person God created you to be— a person who chooses to be good.

6. Ask the participants the following questions:

- How do we reconcile our relationship with God?
- Would the figure look the same if I were to remove the tape?

In the discussion, refer to the bullet points below, which are taken from pages 183–186 of the *CFH:*

- The sacrament of Penance and Reconciliation is primarily concerned with spiritual healing.
- Conversion is the turning away from sin and the turning toward God that happens through the sacrament. Through conversion we recover the grace we lost through turning away from God's love.
- Through the sacrament we are reconciled with God and with the Church, the Body of Christ. Our relationships with other Christians are restored, although we may still need to seek forgiveness from those who were directly affected by our sin.

VARIATION:
Gender-Specific Groups

Provide the participants with the questions in step 6, and invite them to work in small, gender-specific groups to find the answers in *The Catholic Faith Handbook for Youth.* Have each group share its answers. Then post the answers on newsprint.

celebrate this relationship. Then ask them to imagine that their beloved spouse is unfaithful. How do they feel? The Bible frequently uses this experience of marital infidelity (unfaithfulness) as a metaphor to describe how God feels when the people are unfaithful to God's laws. The Book of Hosea contains an extended treatment of this metaphor.

- **Not two but one.** Have the participants read the article "The Theology of Sexuality," on page 267 of *The Catholic Faith Handbook for Youth*. Invite them to make a list of the many ways in which two people become one in a sacramental marriage. How else does this becoming one show up in the couple's everyday life?

Respecting Sexuality: The Challenge of Sexuality

This session covers some elements of pages 265–275 of *The Catholic Faith Handbook for Youth*. Chapter 7 covers other topics from these pages. For further exploration, check out paragraph numbers 2351–2359, 2376–2391, 2396, 2399–2400, 2514–2516, 2525–2526, and 2528–2530 of the *Catechism of the Catholic Church*.

Session Summary

- Both the Scriptures and Tradition begin with the basic teaching that sexuality is one of God's greatest and most beautiful gifts to us.
- The sixth (You shall not commit adultery.) and ninth (You shall not covet your neighbor's wife.) commandments simply remind us that the misuse of such a great gift can cause great harm.
- Adding to the problem is that the gift of sex has become a marketing tool to sell products—jeans, perfume, soft drinks, shoes, and cars—even appliances.
- Why does the Church make such a big deal out of sex belonging only in marriage? To answer that question, we need to look at how God made the act of sexual intercourse different for humans than for any other species. Simply stated, God made sex for three purposes:
  - Sex creates new life.
  - Sex expresses loving union.
  - Sex brings us joy and pleasure.
- If sex was only about experiencing pleasure, we would be more like animals than humans. People who have sex just because it feels good are missing the point. They are acting on instinct—body only, no heart or head involved.
- The ninth commandment, "You shall not covet your neighbor's wife," is closely related to the sixth commandment against adultery. It speaks of lust and carnal concupiscence. These intimidating words simply mean that the life forces within us have a dark side. Men often experience this dark side as an overwhelming desire for sexual pleasure. Women often experience it as a need to have sex in order to hold on to a relationship.
- The gift the Holy Spirit gives us to keep our desires in check is the virtue called temperance. Temperance is about using our will to overcome our instincts.

- The demons of the dark side will always be present, threatening our good intentions. Fornication is a biblical term that refers to sex outside of marriage. Television shows may influence you to think that casual sex is a sign of the times, and that everybody is doing it, but the reality is that more and more teenagers are questioning the wisdom of sex without permanent commitment. Recent studies show that the majority of adolescents who have had sex, said they wish they had waited.

- Masturbation, genital activity alone or with another person that does not result in sexual intercourse, is also a sin against chastity. It is all about pleasure without regard for life or real love. Sins against chastity include other forms of genital sexual activity that stop short of sexual intercourse, such as petting or oral sex. They are forms of exploitation, and are not appropriate sexual expressions for semicommitted love.

- One of the most common offenses against the sixth and ninth commandments is pornography. The Internet has made this evil more accessible to young people. Pornography is dangerous because it violates human dignity. It takes the gift of sexuality and makes it an object to be exploited and abused.

- The issue of homosexuality is an especially difficult one in our discussion of sexuality. For reasons that are still unclear, some people experience a strong sexual attraction toward persons of the same sex.

- The Catholic Church affirms that people with a homosexual orientation are children of God, and must be treated with respect, compassion, and sensitivity. It is never moral to discriminate, act violently toward, make jokes about, or look down on them.

- Although the Church is clear about accepting our homosexual brothers and sisters—that is, gay men and lesbian women—as part of the Body of Christ, she also teaches that homosexual acts are against natural law because they do not allow for the possibility of life.

- All of us are called to practice chastity according to our station in life.

- For those who realize that they are sexually attracted to people of the same sex, avoiding genital sexual expression can be a cross to bear, requiring great effort at mastering will over instinct.

- An active prayer life and support from others within the faith community can help men and women with homosexual orientations to accept the gift of their sexuality through deepening friendships that are a sign of Christian love.

(All summary points are taken from *The Catholic Faith Handbook for Youth,* by Brian Singer-Towns et al. [Winona, MN: Saint Mary's Press, 2004], pages 266–273. Copyright © 2004 by Saint Mary's Press. All rights reserved.)

Talk Points

- In what ways can you control the degree of influence that the media's sexual values exert over you?
- In what ways can you get involved in activities with young people who are finding healthy, wholesome ways of enjoying one another's company without tempting sexual involvement before marriage?
- Are there sexual dangers, such as pornography, the depiction of sexuality on television, in-vitro fertilization, or artificial insemination, about which you feel strongly enough to take political action?

Respecting Material Goods

AT A GLANCE

Study It

Core Session

◆ Is It Stealing?
(45 minutes)

Session Extensions

◆ Living in a Material World
(20 minutes)

◆ Help Wanted
(20 minutes)

Pray It

◆ Knowing Jesus in Those in Need
(10 minutes)

Live It

◆ Simple living
◆ Organizations that help
◆ Preferential option for the poor
◆ Advertising envy

Overview

Respecting material goods pertains to the seventh and tenth commandments. This session explores how those commandments apply to the life that young people are leading or will lead in the future. In addition to emphasizing respect both for the goods of others and for the earth's resources, which benefit all people, this session explores the social doctrine of the Church, the application of these principles to our vocation and our work, and the proper use of wealth.

Outcomes

◆ The learner will understand the Church's teaching on the seventh commandment with respect to stealing.
◆ The learner will be aware of the application of the tenth commandment to the dangers of materialism and envy.
◆ The learner will consider the best way to serve God through vocation, work, and wealth.

Background Reading

◆ This session covers pages 276–284 of *The Catholic Faith Handbook for Youth*.
◆ For further exploration, check out paragraph numbers 2401–2463 and 2534–2557 of the *Catechism*.
◆ Scriptural connections: Mark 12:41–44, Luke 21:1–4 (the widow's offering), Acts 4:32—5:11 (stewardship and the withholding by Ananias and Saphira), 1 Tim. 6:6–10 (true riches)
◆ *Catholic Youth Bible* article connections: "The Loaded Question" (Luke 18:18–30), "Stewardship" (Acts 4:32—37), "Dangers of Money" (1 Tim. 6:6–10)

129

Core Session

Is It Stealing? (45 minutes)

Preparation
- Gather the following items:
  - ❑ copies of handout 17, "Respecting Material Goods," one for each participant
  - ❑ paper
  - ❑ pens or pencils
- Review the summary points in step 6 of this session and the relevant material on pages 276–284 of *The Catholic Faith Handbook for Youth (CFH)*. Be prepared to share the information with the young people.

1. Begin the session by dividing the participants into three groups.

2. Explain that they will be presenting common arguments on the morality of downloading music from the Internet without paying the record company for the music.

3. Share the following directions with the small groups:
- Group 1 will take on the role of those who argue that such downloading is not stealing and that downloading music without paying for it is not wrong.
- Group 2 will take on the role of those who argue that such downloading is stealing but is justifiable and morally acceptable.
- Group 3 will argue that such downloading is stealing and morally unacceptable.
- Each group will have 3 minutes to present its argument. The other groups will not respond or interrupt while a group is presenting.
- After all three groups have made their presentations, each group will have 2 minutes to respond to the presentations of the other groups.
- Remind the participants that this exercise is not a debate but a presentation of arguments to support the point of view assigned to each group.

4. Allow the groups 10 minutes to prepare and organize the presentations. Provide them with paper and pens or pencils for writing down the key points of the presentations.

5. Assemble the groups for the presentations. Keep track of time, and ensure that no one interrupts the groups during the presentations. Invite all the groups to keep track of what the other groups are saying so they can respond later. Finally, emphasize that this exercise is not a personal debate; they must stick to the point, present their arguments, and not verbally attack the other groups.

When all three groups have presented their arguments, ask the first two groups the following question:

- Did the third group (the one that represents the Church's view) do an adequate job of presenting its position? If yes, how so? If no, what other thoughts would you add?

6. Following the presentations and the rebuttals, conduct a brief presentation on stealing, using key phrases from the preceding steps and the bullet points below, which are taken from pages 277–278 and 283–284 of the *CFH:*

- Let's start with the basics: "You shall not steal." Anytime we take something that doesn't belong to us without the permission of the rightful owner, it is stealing, and it is a sin—even if the owner never finds out or misses the item.
- If you shoplift and get away with it, you are still guilty of theft. You can tell yourself that the store will never miss it, or that the company makes enough money anyway, but your act is still wrong.
- Stealing ideas or information from others may be more abstract, but it is still wrong. This is a primary reason why cheating—whether on school tests or as a business practice—is sinful. Plagiarism, that is, copying someone else's words or ideas without permission or giving proper credit is a form of stealing; so is pirating music, videos, and software.
- Regardless of the kind of theft, those who take from others damage the harmony of society.
- Stealing requires confession, and reparation (making amends) or restitution (returning what you have stolen). You need to give it back or make it right, and ask for forgiveness.
- The tenth and final commandment, "You shall not covet your neighbor's goods," warns us about the human tendency to want what others have. We overcome that tendency by always acting morally toward others and by learning to be humble.

7. Use the following reflection questions to help the participants understand the topic of stealing from the viewpoint of the Church's teaching.

- In light of the information from the *CFH,* why is illegally downloading music wrong?

Mediaconnections

- Use the Catholic Relief Services (CRS) video segment *To Earn or Learn* (CRS, 1 minute, 26 seconds, undated) to highlight child labor issues in India. This and other film clips are available at *www.catholicrelief.org/newsroom/video/index.cfm*
- Explore the CRS Web site, learn more about the Food Fast program, and decide what your group can do to participate: *www.catholicrelief.org/what_we_do_in_the_united_states/food_fast/index.cfm.*
- Show selected scenes of films with money and greed themes, such as *Trading Places* (Paramount, 118 minutes, 1983, rated R) and *Wall Street* (20th Century Fox, 125 minutes, 1987, rated R). (Obtain parental permission for the participants who are minors to view an R-rated movie, and use your best judgment regarding the appropriateness of the film and the advisability of viewing relevant excerpts.) Invite the participants to discuss how the various messages portrayed relate to the seventh and tenth commandments.

Familyconnections

◆ Invite participants and family members to discuss ways they can simplify their life. Suggest eliminating meat one day a week, planning a family event that doesn't require money, or cutting out electronic entertainment one night a month.

◆ Suggest a family conversation with parents and grandparents about what life was like before computers, cell phones, cable television, color (or any) television, CDs, MP3s, VCRs, tapes, and so on. Ask elderly family members whether they remember life before radio (radio broadcasts in and near the bigger cities began in the early 1920s). Invite the participants to listen with openness for the simple pleasures that their parents and grandparents enjoyed.

◆ Invite participants and families to talk about creating a family foundation. Although the family might not be wealthy enough to fund the foundation with millions of dollars, they probably have some resources (love, time, energy) that can be channeled toward a particular cause. Perhaps the family has an interest in the elderly, the homeless, Bangladesh, or the

• Who gets hurt when you steal music on the Internet?
• Is stealing from someone who is wealthy more justifiable than stealing from a poor person? Why or why not?
• What is the difference, ethically, between stealing a package of chewing gum and stealing a car?
• How does this topic of stealing relate to cheating on a test or copying someone's homework?

8. Conclude this session by reiterating the Church's teaching on stealing. Challenge the participants to be aware of the times when they face options that oppose this moral truth. Be sure to note that the content of this session was drawn from chapter 28 of the *CFH*. Encourage the participants to read and review it in the next few days.

Session Extensions

Living in a Material World (20 minutes)

Preparation
• Gather the following items:
  ❏ copies of handout 18, "Living in a Material World," one for each participant
  ❏ pens or pencils

1. Explain that the participants are going to spend a little time looking at the material goods and the non-material items that they require to be happy.

2. Distribute handout 18 and pens or pencils to the participants, and invite them to take a few moments to fill it out individually.

3. Once everyone has completed the lists, invite the entire group to rank the items in order of importance. Ask for a show of hands for each item. Note that although many participants likely ranked the items about material goods at the bottom of the list when the time came to prioritize it, we cannot ignore basic items such as food and shelter.

4. Conduct a brief presentation on the use of material goods, using key phrases from the core session and the bullet points below, which are taken from pages 279 and 282–284 of the *CFH*:
• The complex problems of economic injustice clearly hurt poor people, but they also wound the hearts of rich people. Having too much can be as bad for us as having too little. A different kind of poverty affects those of us with great material wealth. Poverty of spirit, like material poverty, leads to unhappiness.

- Unfortunately, the "more, more, more" of excess consumerism doesn't make us happy. No matter how many music CDs, computerized gadgets, jeans, or pairs of shoes we have, somebody else is bound to have more than we do. That's where the tenth commandment and envy come in. It is just too easy for us humans to be jealous of our neighbor's things or our neighbor's talents.
- Our first response, if we have the means, is to help ease the hunger or poverty by donating money or food. This is a work of charity (almsgiving, in traditional language).
- Jesus came to bring us life abundant, not in the material sense but in the deep authentic joy of knowing that riches will not make us ultimately happy.

5. Conclude this activity by stressing the importance of recognizing what is a necessity for life and what is a luxury. Difficulties arise when we view luxuries as necessities and covet the luxuries that other people have. We also have to be careful not to value things over people.

Help Wanted (20 minutes)

Preparation
- Gather the following items:
  - ❑ newsprint
  - ❑ markers
  - ❑ the help-wanted section of a Sunday newspaper from the nearest sizable metropolitan area
  - ❑ paper
  - ❑ pens or pencils

1. Begin the session by conducting a brief presentation on the themes of vocation and work, using the bullet points below, which are taken from pages 281–283 of *The Catholic Faith Handbook for Youth*:

- You can see that the seventh commandment has a lot to do with work and jobs. Working and paychecks are one way we participate in the distribution of the world's resources. Our work should be a reflection of who we are as whole persons. Work is part of our vocation, that is, God's call for our purpose in life. Our work should reflect our values, including our religious values.
- As a young person, your call right now is primarily to study and learn, though you may also have other jobs in your family or the community. But as you grow older and find your vocation, the work you do has a higher purpose. By contributing your talents to society, you participate in the work of creation. And when you connect that work with Jesus, you

foster care organization that took such good care of Mom when she was a little girl. Could the family gather all its available money, time, and love (through its foundation) for this cause?

TryThis

Invite the participants to pay particular attention to the advertisements that bombard them daily. Ask them to identify examples that present luxury items as necessities for a happy life.

JournalACTIVITIES

- ◆ Rate yourself as someone who respects material goods. Do you recycle? put things back where you found them? replace what you use of other people's things? give credit to your sources? pay for your music? give to poor people when you can? In which areas could you make some improvement?
- ◆ Make a list of the kinds of things you want to have as an adult. Include the type of house, car, and income you want, and list as many details as you can think of. Next to each item, note whether it is a need or a want. In a third column, write how the item affects the food chain, poor countries, the environment, and poor people locally. Then

determine whether you want to reconsider your lifestyle desires.

◆ Think about what life must be like for a person your age who is a slave right now, somewhere in the world. Girls are enslaved in the sex industry in Southeast Asia; boys are enslaved in Sudan, tending animals and being beaten; boys and girls are enslaved in armies and militias around the world. Write a letter to one of these enslaved teens to explain the things you wish for the person and to offer a reason to hope.

discover that work does not have to be a burden, but part of the process of redemption, our ultimate purpose in life.

• What does all this have to do with the seventh commandment, "You shall not steal"? Employers expect that workers will work to the best of their ability for the wages they are paid. Coming in late, slacking off at work, or leaving early is stealing from the boss and the company. It means others may have to do more than their fair share—plus your employer is not getting her money's worth.

• However, employers have responsibilities too—to pay just wages, provide safe working conditions, and consider the economic and ecological effects on the rest of society. Dumping waste, causing air pollution, and depleting natural resources are all forms of stealing that affect the common good. Good business means that you clean up your mess and put things back where they belong.

2. Explain to the participants that our vocation is how we live out our faith in all aspects of our life. Our work is part of our vocation. Ask them to think about their vocation, their purpose in life. Write some of these vocations on newsprint. Encourage them to focus only on their vocation, their purpose in life, and to leave their ideas about career or job until a later step.

3. Then distribute pages of the Sunday help-wanted section to the participants. Instruct them to read some of the large display ads at the top rather than the small classified ads at the bottom. Ask them to analyze the ads for whether the employers are trying to appeal to the job hunters' sense of purpose in life. What other factors are employers emphasizing to attract potential workers? Do these other factors conflict with the vocation element or make it easier to fulfill a vocation?

4. Distribute paper and pens or pencils. Invite the participants to think about a career they have considered and to write a help-wanted ad that would let them do the job they want and also fulfill their vocation.

5. Invite all or a few participants to share their help-wanted ads with the whole group. To close, encourage them to keep the ads so that when they are looking for purposeful work someday, they will recall the ad for the ideal job.

Knowing Jesus in Those in Need (10 minutes)

Preparation

- Gather the following items:
  - ❑ a *Catholic Youth Bible* or other Bible, opened to Matt. 25:31–46
  - ❑ copies of the prayer on resource 4, "Knowing Jesus in Those in Need," one for each participant
  - ❑ six life-size photos of faces of people in need, as mentioned in the prayer on resource 4 (possible sources: *National Geographic* or the Internet), copied and enlarged to the proper size
  - ❑ a tape player or a CD player
  - ❑ a song from *Spirit & Song* Connections or an alternative song that reflects the theme of care of the poor
- Arrange the space so that the participants can sit facing inward and in a circle.
- Recruit six volunteers to carry the six photos around the circle to show them to the participants.

1. Ask a participant to prepare to read aloud Matt. 25:31–46 at the appropriate time.

2. Distribute a copy of the prayer on resource 4 to each of the participants, and ask them to sit in a circle.

3. Invite the participants to enter into prayer. Encourage them to pray for the person whose picture a participant is carrying around the circle and for other people who face similar needs and challenges. After everyone has seen the first picture, ask the participants to pray aloud the first line of the prayer on the resource. Continue this format with the second picture and the second line of the prayer, and so on, until all six pictures have circled the group.

4. After the sixth picture and the sixth line of the prayer, invite the selected reader to stand and proclaim the reading from Matt. 25:31–46.

5. After a brief pause, invite the participants to pray the last line of the prayer on the resource.

6. Play the selected song, and ask the six participants to carry the pictures around the circle again.

(This prayer service is adapted from the article "Prayer to Know Jesus in Those in Need," in Brian Singer-Towns, *The Catholic Faith Handbook for Youth*, p. 281.)

Spirit & Song connections

- "Open My Eyes, Lord," by Jesse Manibusan
- "Christ, Be Our Light," by Bernadette Farrell
- "The Cry of the Poor," by John Foley, SJ
- "The Summons, a Scottish Traditional Tune," by John L. Bell, arranged by Bobby Fisher

Options and Actions

- **Simple living.** Invite the participants to read the article "Simple Living," on page 279 in *The Catholic Faith Handbook for Youth (CFH)*. Ask them to brainstorm what they can do to live more simply. Invite all to commit to one change to simplify the way they live.

- **Organizations that help.** The saintly profile on page 283 of the *CFH* describes the society founded in Saint Vincent de Paul's honor. Can you find organizations in your area that help channel the energy of donors and volunteers to the people who need assistance?

- **Preferential option for the poor.** The article on page 284 of the *CFH* explains the Church's position that when we have a choice, we ought to exercise a preferential option for the poor. Invite the participants to discuss some important local, state, or national political or social topic and to decide which result would express a preferential option for the poor. Invite the participants to take action (write a letter to the editor, to a legislator or city councilor, and so forth) that encourages the political or social agency to do the right thing.

- **Advertising envy.** Ask participants how many advertisements they see in a day that encourage them to want what their neighbors have. If wanting what our neighbors have is a violation of the ninth commandment ("You shall not covet . . . anything that belongs to your neighbor," Exodus 20:17), why do so many companies encourage it? They want to motivate people to spend their wealth with the company rather than with someone else. Invite the participants to brainstorm ideas for resisting the "more, more, more" of our consumer society. Ask them to adopt one strategy for the week ahead.

Respecting Material Goods

This session covers pages 276–284 of *The Catholic Faith Handbook for Youth*. For further exploration, check out paragraph numbers 2401–2463 and 2534–2557 of the *Catechism of the Catholic Church*.

Session Summary

- Let's start with the basics: "You shall not steal." Anytime we take something that doesn't belong to us without the permission of the rightful owner, it is stealing, and it is a sin—even if the owner never finds out or misses the item.

- If you shoplift and get away with it, you are still guilty of theft. You can tell yourself that the store will never miss it, or that the company makes enough money anyway, but your act is still wrong.

- Stealing ideas or information from others may be more abstract, but it is still wrong. This is a primary reason why cheating—whether on school tests or as a business practice—is sinful. Plagiarism, that is, copying someone else's words or ideas without permission or giving proper credit, is a form of stealing; so is pirating music, videos, and software.

- Regardless of the kind of theft, those who take from others damage the harmony of society.

- Stealing requires confession, and reparation (making amends) or restitution (returning what you have stolen). You need to give it back or make it right, and ask for forgiveness.

- You can see that the seventh commandment has a lot to do with work and jobs. Working and paychecks are one way we participate in the distribution of the world's resources. Our work should be a reflection of who we are as whole persons. Work is part of our vocation, that is, God's call for our purpose in life. Our work should reflect our values, including our religious values.

- The complex problems of economic injustice clearly hurt poor people, but they also wound the hearts of rich people. Having too much can be as bad for us as having too little. A different kind of poverty affects those of us with great material wealth. Poverty of spirit, like material poverty, leads to unhappiness.

- Unfortunately, the "more, more, more" of excess consumerism doesn't make us happy. No matter how many music CDs, computerized gadgets, jeans, or pairs of shoes we have, somebody else is bound to have more than we do. That's where the tenth commandment and envy come in. It is just too easy for us humans to be jealous of our neighbor's things or our neighbor's talents.
- Our first response, if we have the means, is to help ease the hunger or poverty by donating money or food. This is a work of charity (almsgiving, in traditional language).
- Jesus came to bring us life abundant, not in the material sense but in the deep authentic joy of knowing that riches will not make us ultimately happy.
- The tenth and final commandment, "You shall not covet your neighbor's goods," warns us about the human tendency to want what others have. We overcome that tendency by always acting morally toward others and by learning to be humble.

(All summary points are taken from *The Catholic Faith Handbook for Youth,* by Brian Singer-Towns et al. [Winona, MN: Saint Mary's Press, 2004], pages 277–284. Copyright © 2004 by Saint Mary's Press. All rights reserved.)

Talk Points

- How can you be more aware of the power of advertising in your life? Make a list of all the commercials and ads you saw last week.
- Think about the things you have purchased recently. How many of them did you need for basic survival? How can you make good buying decisions in the future?
- Pope Paul VI said, "If you want peace, work for justice." How does injustice lead to conflict? Can you think of examples within your own family, your community, and the world where conflict resulted from an injustice?

Living in a Material World

Numerically rank the following items (1 being most important) on their necessity for living a happy life. To the right of each item, write whether the item is a luxury or a necessity.

_____ top-of-the-line automobile   _____

_____ loving parents   _____

_____ good stereo equipment   _____

_____ your own bedroom   _____

_____ food   _____

_____ good friends   _____

_____ shelter   _____

_____ clean air   _____

_____ happiness   _____

_____ health insurance   _____

_____ brand-name shoes   _____

_____ extra spending money   _____

_____ a fashionable wardrobe   _____

_____ substantial money in savings   _____

_____ health   _____

_____ a ski vacation   _____

_____ a spiritual life   _____

_____ money for college   _____

_____ emotional stability   _____

_____ jewelry   _____

_____ contributions to the Church   _____

Knowing Jesus in Those in Need

1. Jesus, open my eyes to see you in the faces of people who are poor and who suffer from injustice in our world.

2. Open my hands in service to people who are hungry and thirsty.

3. Warm my heart to welcome you in the immigrant, the refugee, and people who feel all alone.

4. Grant me a spirit of simplicity in my life so that more resources will be available to clothe the naked.

5. Soften my heart with compassion for people who are ill and lack basic medical care.

6. Move my feet on the path of action for the least of your people.

7. Give me the joy and the deep peace of your presence as I serve you in my brothers and sisters in need. Amen.

(This prayer is taken from *The Catholic Faith Handbook for Youth,* by Brian Singer-Towns et al. [Winona, MN: Saint Mary's Press, 2004], page 281. Copyright © 2004 by Saint Mary's Press. All rights reserved.)

--✂

1. Jesus, open my eyes to see you in the faces of people who are poor and who suffer from injustice in our world.

2. Open my hands in service to people who are hungry and thirsty.

3. Warm my heart to welcome you in the immigrant, the refugee, and people who feel all alone.

4. Grant me a spirit of simplicity in my life so that more resources will be available to clothe the naked.

5. Soften my heart with compassion for people who are ill and lack basic medical care.

6. Move my feet on the path of action for the least of your people.

7. Give me the joy and the deep peace of your presence as I serve you in my brothers and sisters in need. Amen.

(This prayer is taken from *The Catholic Faith Handbook for Youth,* by Brian Singer-Towns et al. [Winona, MN: Saint Mary's Press, 2004], page 281. Copyright © 2004 by Saint Mary's Press. All rights reserved.)

10 Respecting Truth

Overview

Truth is an aspect of the Catholic moral life that presents challenges every day. Many people encourage the young to cheat, plagiarize, gossip, bend the truth, and violate confidences. This session explores the eighth commandment and its relation to the daily life of young people and the influence of the media. The session stresses the harm that failure to tell the truth can cause and the power that words have.

Outcomes

◆ The learner will understand the importance of truth and the harm of lying.

◆ The learner will experience the power of words to make or break confidences and reputations.

◆ The learner will realize how important a foundation of truth is for society and how necessary reparations are when truth is violated.

Background Reading

◆ This session covers pages 285–293 of *The Catholic Faith Handbook for Youth*.

◆ For further exploration, check out paragraph numbers 2464–2513 of the *Catechism*.

◆ Scriptural connections: Gen. 4:9 (Cain denies that he knows Abel's whereabouts.), Sir. 27:16–21 (betraying secrets), John 8:31–32 (The truth will make you free.), John 14:6–7 (the way, the truth, and the life), James 3:1–12 (taming the tongue)

◆ *Catholic Youth Bible* article connections: "Integrity and Values" (Psalm 26), "Nothing but the Truth" (Prov. 10:18–21), "The Holy Spirit Guides Us into All Truth!" (John 14:15–31; 16:5–15)

Study It

Core Session

◆ Truth Woven into the Fabric of Life
(45 minutes)

Session Extensions

◆ The Power of Speech
(20 minutes)

◆ Walking in the Truth
(20 minutes)

Pray It

◆ Praying for Strength
(20 minutes)

Live It

◆ Examining hypocrisy

◆ Where kindness and truth meet

◆ The truth that lies behind

◆ Which version is true?

Core Session

Truth Woven into the Fabric of Life (45 minutes)

Preparation

- Gather the following items:
  - ❏ copies of handout 19, "Respecting Truth," one for each participant
  - ❏ paper
  - ❏ pens or pencils
  - ❏ newsprint
  - ❏ markers
- Review the summary points in step 3 of this session and the relevant material on pages 285–293 of *The Catholic Faith Handbook for Youth (CFH)*. Be prepared to share the information with the young people.

1. Form the participants into groups of four. Ask the groups to create a description of a world in which no one can trust anyone else, honesty is not a value, and people and institutions say and do whatever serves their immediate interests. Assign each group one of the following categories:

- friendship
- education
- family relationships
- medical care
- buying or selling goods and services
- sports
- news reporting in the media
- government
- financial institutions
- relations between nations

Provide a few sheets of paper and a pen or pencil to each group. Ask the group to designate a recorder. The task of each group is to create a short story that is based on the group's assigned category about a world without trust. Allow 10 minutes for each group to create its presentation. Have one person from each group come forward and present the story.

2. Lead the participants in a large-group discussion, using the following questions:

- Which stories resemble the world as we know it?
- Why do you think that honesty is such an underemphasized value?
- What do you think Jesus would say about the lack of trust and honesty in our world today?

3. Conduct a presentation on truth using the bullet points below, which are taken from pages 286–291 of the *CFH,* and illustrating them with examples from the participants' stories:

- The eighth commandment, "You shall not bear false witness against your neighbor," includes the sins of lying, deception, hypocrisy, and slander. But the heart of the commandment isn't about forbidding certain acts; it is about being a person of integrity who respects and lives the truth.
- Fortunately, by nature we are inclined toward the truth. Morally we are obliged to seek the truth, especially religious truth. And once we know what is true, we must live by it. Jesus tells us that he is the way, the truth, and the life (John 14:6). As followers of Jesus, we are bound by the truth of the Gospel.
- Because we as humans have a natural tendency to tell the truth, we have to be motivated to tell a lie. Some people lie to cover up something they did wrong; some lie to avoid punishment; others lie to make themselves appear more important. Well-meaning people sometimes lie to avoid confronting someone with an unpleasant truth.
- Getting away with a lie can still hurt and wound others, even if they never find out that you lied to them.
- Spreading a negative rumor about someone never serves any good purpose. And if you pass on or create a rumor or story that is not true, you are "bearing false witness against your neighbor," an even more serious sin called calumny, or slander.
- We are morally obligated to make reparation, or amends, for sins against the truth. Owning up to our lies may be more difficult than telling the truth in the first place. But we must try to undo the harm we have caused.
- Sometimes it is inappropriate to reveal the truth to someone who asks for it. The welfare and safety of others, respect for privacy, and the common good are sufficient reasons for being silent or discreet about the truth.
- Sometimes confidentiality requires secrecy.
- Telling the truth is as important in society as it is among individuals. We need to be able to trust other people in our community and beyond.

4. Ask the participants to suggest the possible cost of honesty. For example, honesty can be costly because of criticism, punishment, and so forth. Print the responses on newsprint. Then ask the participants to name the harms associated with dishonesty, and print these on the newsprint. With the participants, compare and contrast the cost of honesty and the harm of dishonesty.

Mediaconnections

◆ View a television situation comedy to see what kind of honesty or dishonesty it portrays. Then discuss what your observations suggest about the images of lying that TV shows convey.

◆ Conduct a search for fun quizzes and tests on the Internet by using the keywords "honesty," "character," or "integrity" plus the word "quiz."

◆ Listen to a political speech, either a contemporary one or a famous one from history, while reading a transcript of it. Which statements sound untrue? Does the way the politician says something affect whether people accept it as truth? Which statements seem true at the time but later prove to be false? What difference would this reaction have made on the speech's effectiveness?

Familyconnections

◆ Send home colorful adhesive bandages with the participants, at least two for every person in the family. Invite family members to talk about how they have been hurt by the words of another member of the family or how they wonder, after the fact, whether words they spoke have hurt another in the family. Invite the family to describe in detail how the incident felt. For situations in which people are willing to acknowledge the hurt, apologize, forgive, and use the adhesive bandage as a symbol of the reconciliation.

◆ Invite family members to talk about one of the family's secrets and to discuss why it is a secret. Often young people have trouble understanding why their parents want them to keep secret from their friends some aspect of the family's history. If the older members can explain why the fact is a secret, the younger members will have a reason to keep it confidential.

5. Ask the participants to suggest the benefits of honesty. Print the responses on newsprint. Then ask the participants to name the benefits that people often presume they will get by being dishonest, such as avoiding embarrassment, not hurting others, passing a test, getting a good grade, and getting someone to like them. Print those presumed benefits on the newsprint. With the participants, compare and contrast the benefits of honesty and the hoped-for benefits of dishonesty.

6. Invite the participants to return to their small groups. Using their pen or pencil and paper, the groups should develop some suggestions for how the characters in their earlier story might change by moving from a world of no honesty to a world of honesty. How can the characters make amends for the harm they caused in the old world?

7. Invite the participants to consider whether in their own life they can use the suggestions for repairing the harm in their story world. Conclude the session by inviting a few participants to share their action steps for living a more truth-filled life. Finally, be sure to note that the content of this session was drawn from chapter 29 of the *CFH*. Encourage the participants to read and review it in the next few days.

Session Extensions

The Power of Speech (20 minutes)

Preparation

• Gather the following items:
  ❏ a *Catholic Youth Bible* or other Bible, opened to James 3:1–12
  ❏ newsprint
  ❏ marker
  ❏ paper, one sheet for each participant
  ❏ pens or pencils

1. Ask a volunteer to read James 3:1–12 to the group. Have another volunteer read the article "The Tongue: Friend or Foe?" near James 3:1–12 in the *CYB*.

2. Invite the participants to brainstorm the different ways in which our speech can hurt others. List their responses on newsprint. Then ask them to name different ways in which the spoken word can heal or help others. List their insights on the newsprint.

3. Divide the participants into groups of four. Give each person a sheet of paper and a pen or pencil. Give them the following instructions:

- The youngest person in the group sits facing away from the group, and the other group members take turns naming three things they like about the person.
- The person being affirmed writes down these positive comments.
- Then the next youngest person takes a turn listening to positive statements, and so on, until the group has affirmed everyone.
- Be positive and affirming in this exercise.
- Avoid saying anything that might embarrass or hurt someone.

4. In summary, lead the group in suggesting general guidelines that might help them and their friends use the gift of speech well. A few examples will get them started:

- Keep gossip out of your everyday conversations. Gossip is an easy way for you to tear down the dignity and reputation of another person.
- When you say something nice to another person, be specific in your affirmation. Say, "I like how you helped Heather work out that algebra problem," rather than, "You're good in math."
- Think before you speak. Sometimes saying the first thing that comes to mind is the last thing you should say!
- Be careful with the words you use. Some words are hurtful, whether you mean them or not. Say to yourself, "How would I feel if someone said that to me?"
- Know what is the best time to tell another person something that might be hard to accept. Do it in private.
- When you make a mistake and hurt someone by what you said, apologize! Asking for forgiveness is a sign of a maturing Christian.

(This activity is adapted from Christine Schmertz Navarro et al., *Teaching Activities Manual for "The Catholic Youth Bible,"* pp. 307–308.)

Walking in the Truth (20 minutes)

Preparation
- Gather the following items:
  - ❑ *Catholic Youth Bibles* or other Bibles, one for each pair of participants
  - ❑ newsprint
  - ❑ markers
  - ❑ scissors

1. Ask the participants to find a partner. Distribute a Bible to each pair. Refer the participants to the letters found in 2 John and 3 John. Tell them to pay special attention to the author's focus on "walking in the truth." Have each pair read both letters.

2. Provide each pair with a sheet of newsprint, a marker, and scissors. Invite the pairs to trace a pair of feet (the left foot of one person and the

JournalACTIVITIES

- Compose a response you could use when you hear someone gossiping.
- What are some things you have told yourself in the past that you now recognize as untrue?
- Spend some time reflecting on this quote: "This is where honesty, truth-telling, and realness begin. Not with the revelation or the uncovering of dramatic deceptions and secrets, but rather with the dailiness of what we call "being oneself." (Harriet G. Lerner, quoted in Shelley Tucker, comp., *Openings,* p. 19.)
- Have you ever had to make a decision about revealing someone's secret—for their own good? What were the circumstances? How did you handle it? Do you wish you had done anything differently? (*CFH,* p. 292)

right foot of the other person) on newsprint and to cut out the footprints. On one partner's footprint, write statements from the Scripture passages that explain the concept of walking in the truth. For example, walking in the truth means that we must love one another (2 John, chap. 5); walking in the truth means knowing and doing what is right and good; actions must match knowledge (3 John, chap. 11). On the other partner's footprint, write her or his interpretation of this concept. For example, being a disciple of Jesus means trying to show unconditional love to everyone I meet; I must "walk the talk"; knowing what is good is not enough, for I must also do good.

3. Once the pairs have completed their tasks, ask them to place the footprints on the floor one after the other, as though they were creating a path. Ask the participants to look at the footprints and discuss the various interpretations that are written on them. Discuss the challenges and rewards of looking for "the truth." Ask the question, "How can we recognize the truth?"

(This activity is adapted from Christine Schmertz Navarro et al., *Teaching Activities Manual for "The Catholic Youth Bible,"* pp. 314–315.)

Praying for Strength (20 minutes)

Preparation
- Gather the following items:
  - ❏ a *Catholic Youth Bible* or other Bible
  - ❏ a large candle
  - ❏ a bowl of sand
  - ❏ taper candles, one for each participant
  - ❏ a tape player or a CD player
  - ❏ small slips of paper, one for each participant
  - ❏ pens
- Choose an opening song with a theme of reconciliation, and use "This Little Light of Mine" (or a similar hymn) as the closing song.
- Make three copies of resource 5, "Blessed Are You." Recruit three volunteers to do a reading.
- Set up a prayer space with the large candle, the Bible marked at Ps. 119:41–48 and John 8:31–32, and a bowl of sand with taper candles placed around it. Set the tape or CD player to the appropriate song.
- Distribute a slip of paper and a pen to each participant.

1. Begin the prayer with the sign of the cross. Play the opening song you have selected.

2. Invite the first volunteer to proclaim Ps. 119:41–48. Allow a few moments for quiet reflection. Then ask the second volunteer to proclaim John 8:31–32. Allow a few moments for quiet reflection again, and then offer the following comments in these or your own words:

- In the first reading, the psalmist is asking the Lord for protection from those who would taunt the author for speaking the truth.
- In the reading from John's Gospel, we hear the familiar saying, "The truth will make you free."
- On your slip of paper, write down something about which you are currently struggling to be truthful.
- Then write a short prayer asking God to give you the strength to be truthful. When you're finished, fold your slip of paper in half.

Allow a few minutes for the participants to complete their task.

3. Invite the third volunteer to read "Blessed Are You," from resource 5. Allow a few moments for silent reflection.

4. Invite the participants to place their slips of paper in the empty basket, and tell them that doing so symbolizes placing the request before God. After they place a slip of paper in the basket, invite them to light a taper from the Paschal candle. Tell them that doing so is a sign of taking the light of Christ with them. Tear into small pieces the slips of paper in the basket, while telling the participants that only the individual and God know the requests, which are confidential.

5. Conclude the prayer by playing or singing a final song.

Options and Actions

- **Examining hypocrisy.** Ask the participants to brainstorm examples of hypocrisy. Have them use their examples to create a definition of hypocrisy.
- **Where kindness and truth meet.** Suggest that the participants interview someone they consider to be tactful. Ask them to inquire about any dilemma this person has faced in trying to combine kindness and truth. Then have the group share the stories they heard, but do not identify the person they interviewed.

- **The truth that lies behind.** Ask the participants to read the article "Copy and Paste: An Instant-Messenger Conversation," on page 291 of *The Catholic Faith Handbook for Youth.* Have them discuss how often such half-truths and gossip occur in conversations among their peers. Is it possible to change this habit? Have them rewrite the conversation, as the article suggests at the end. Ask them whether seeing the rewritten conversation opens the possibility that the practice can change.

- **Which version is true?** Ask the participants to watch different versions of the same news story on four national TV networks on the same night. This can be tricky to time, but doable if cable networks are included. Advise the participants to notice the mood, the tone, the attitude, the details included, the predictions made, the causes or reasons offered, and any other striking details. In their opinion, which version comes closest to the truth? Why? What influences their choice: the way the story was presented or their degree of trust in that particular network?

Respecting Truth

This session covers pages 285–293 of *The Catholic Faith Handbook for Youth.* For further exploration, check out paragraph numbers 2464–2513 of the *Catechism of the Catholic Church.*

Session Summary

- The eighth commandment, "You shall not bear false witness against your neighbor," includes the sins of lying, deception, hypocrisy, and slander. But the heart of the commandment isn't about forbidding certain acts; it is about being a person of integrity who respects and lives the truth.
- Fortunately, by nature we are inclined toward the truth. Morally we are obliged to seek the truth, especially religious truth. And once we know what is true, we must live by it. Jesus tells us that he is the way, the truth, and the life (John 14:6, NRSV). As followers of Jesus, we are bound by the truth of the Gospel.
- Because we as humans have a natural tendency to tell the truth, we have to be motivated to tell a lie. Some people lie to cover up something they did wrong; some lie to avoid punishment; others lie to make themselves appear more important. Well-meaning people sometimes lie to avoid confronting someone with an unpleasant truth.
- Getting away with a lie can still hurt and wound others, even if they never find out that you lied to them.
- Spreading a negative rumor about someone never serves any good purpose. And if you pass on or create a rumor or story that is not true, you are "bearing false witness against your neighbor," an even more serious sin called calumny, or slander.
- We are morally obligated to make reparation, or amends, for sins against the truth. Owning up to our lies may be more difficult than telling the truth in the first place. But we must try to undo the harm we have caused.
- Sometimes it is inappropriate to reveal the truth to someone who asks for it. The welfare and safety of others, respect for privacy, and the common good are sufficient reasons for being silent or discreet about the truth.
- Sometimes confidentiality requires secrecy.
- Telling the truth is as important in society as it is among individuals. We need to be able to trust other people in our community and beyond.

    (All summary points are taken from *The Catholic Faith Handbook for Youth,* by Brian Singer-Towns et al. [Winona, MN: Saint Mary's Press, 2004], pages 285–293. Copyright © 2004 by Saint Mary's Press. All rights reserved.)

Talk Points

- Talk about an incident, either in your own life or in someone else's, in which a person spun a web of lies. How did the web become a trap for the person telling the lies?
- What are a few ways in which you can become more honest with yourself?
- For two days, keep track on paper of a situation in which telling a white lie seems like the obvious or easiest thing for you to do.
- Talk about the kinds of information you usually count on as being true; in other words, this information, if false, would mess up your life or your plans.

Blessed Are You

Blessed Are You Who Are Meek,
You Shall Have the Earth for Your Inheritance

And to the meek, I said:
Tell me about this beatitude
It doesn't sound like a blessing
To me, it looks like the face of weakness.

A face out in the crowd of lowly ones
shone forth with strength
Her smile reached the door of my heart.
Then this lowly one spoke,

To be meek is to be so full of truth
that everyone is comfortable
in your presence.
It is to have a spirit young as the dawn
a heart old as the evening.
It is to know yourself so well
and live yourself so fully
that your very presence
calls forth gifts in others.
It is to be comfortable
with your anger
and with your compassion.

The meek one drew silent for a moment.
Then lifting her eyes, she said:

When you are meek
you don't need a lot of followers
you just need a lot of truth.

The lowly ones are able
to stand out in the open and speak the truth
sometimes quietly
sometimes loudly.
The truth will be spoken
even if no one listens
even if no one hears.
For the meek person doesn't need followers
The meek need to be true to themselves.

No greater truth was ever spoken.
The meek shall inherit the earth.

(This prayer is quoted from *Seasons of Your Heart: Prayers and Reflections,* by Macrina Wiederkehr [New York: HarperCollins, 1991], pages 99–100. Copyright © 1991 by Macrina Wiederkehr. All rights reserved. Used with permission.)

The Moral Life

Overview

No program on morality would be complete without a session on the virtues, on forgiveness, and on grace. Young people today need both the theological virtues, which bring them God's support and comfort, and the cardinal virtues, the tool belt that equips them for life. This session also covers forgiveness and grace, which support us in our moral life.

Outcomes

◆ The learner will understand and learn how to cultivate the cardinal virtues: prudence, justice, temperance, and fortitude.
◆ The learner will understand the value and the source of the theological virtues: faith, hope, and charity.
◆ The learner will appreciate the meaning and importance of forgiveness and grace in living a Christian moral life.

Background Reading

◆ This session covers pages 294–301 of *The Catholic Faith Handbook for Youth.*
◆ For further exploration, check out paragraph numbers 1803–1829, 1833–1844, and 1987–2029 of the *Catechism.*
◆ Scriptural connections: Gen. 12:1—25:11 (the faith of Abraham and Sarah), Neh., chap. 4 (Nehemiah faces hostility.), Rom. 3:21–31 (righteousness through faith), 1 Cor., chap. 13 (the gift of love)
◆ *Catholic Youth Bible* article connections: "Introducing Abraham and Sarah" (Gen. 12:1), Nehemiah's Strength (Neh. 4), "Hope for the Faithful" (Tob., chap. 13), "The Law, Faith, and Salvation" (Rom. 3:21–31), "Trusting the Grace of God" (Rom. 5:1–11), "Hope" (Rom. 8:18–30), "God's Love" (1 Cor. 13)

Core Session

Virtue–al Reality (45 minutes)

Preparation

- Gather the following items:
  - ❑ copies of handout 20, "The Moral Life," one for each participant
  - ❑ copies of handout 21, "Virtue–al Reality," one for each of the four small groups
  - ❑ paper
  - ❑ pens or pencils
  - ❑ newsprint
  - ❑ markers
- Review the summary points in step 5 of this session and the relevant material on pages 294–301 of *The Catholic Faith Handbook for Youth (CFH)*. Be prepared to share the information with the young people.

   1. Begin by forming the participants into four groups.

   2. Explain that they are participants on a new reality television show called "Virtue–al Reality." Each group focuses on a situation they might encounter on a Friday evening and determines what risks, temptations, and moral dilemmas its members might face in a given scenario. The group then drafts a plan of action to help its members counter these risks, temptations, and moral dilemmas before they occur.

   3. Assign one of the following Friday-night scenarios to each group:
- A group of friends is going to the mall.
- A group of friends is going to a party.
- A group of friends is going to a school sporting event.
- A group of friends is going to a sci-fi film at the local cinema.

   4. Distribute paper, pens or pencils, and handout 21 to the four groups. Have one person in each group read that group's scenario aloud to the group members. Ask the members of each group to make a list of the risks, temptations, and moral dilemmas they might face in their group's scenario. Allow 5 to 7 minutes for this step.

   5. Invite the participants to keep these risks in mind during the session. Conduct a brief presentation on the moral life, using the bullet points below, which are taken from pages 295–298 of the *CFH:*

Mediaconnections

◆ Invite the participants to watch an episode of *Seventh Heaven*. Have them identify the moments of grace in the program. Ask them to discuss whether they are aware when similar moments of grace happen in their own life.

◆ Watch the film *Snow White and the Seven Dwarfs* (Walt Disney, 83 minutes, 1937, rated G). Have participants identify which virtues are most prominent in every character, including each dwarf. Ask whether life today is hard to live as virtuously as this movie portrays.

◆ Invite the participants to bring in recordings of the top ten songs on the charts. Analyze whether each song promotes one or more virtues.

- In the moral life, our heart tells us we want to learn to dance the right way, God's way. We have to use our head to learn the meaning of the commandments, which are the basic steps. We listen to the Beatitudes, which are the music that makes the steps come alive. But to best practice the moral life, we have to tap into the gifts God has placed within each one of us: the virtues, forgiveness, and grace.

- Virtues harness the good energy within us. They are habits that we develop over time to help us make good decisions. Like mastering skills in any sport, virtues capitalize on the abilities God has already placed within us.

- When virtues become natural to us, we don't always have to think about the mechanics of moral decision-making.

- There are two kinds of virtues—cardinal virtues and theological virtues. The cardinal virtues come with being human, regardless of religious belief. Jesus was a model for living the four virtues of prudence, justice, temperance, and fortitude. As you develop these four virtues in your life, you become a person of moral character. To have character means that you do the right thing, even under difficult circumstances.

- Prudence is the opposite of being impulsive. Acting impulsively is okay when you are two years old. It may even be appropriate in certain settings that call for creativity or spontaneity. But making moral decisions impulsively can get you into trouble. Prudence requires that you approach moral problems with a degree of caution. Also called wise judgment, prudence relies heavily on our reason. Prudence helps you to stop and think before you act.

- Justice is the virtue concerned with giving both God and neighbor what is their due. It is the habit of thinking about the needs of others as much as your own needs, and acting on what you know to be fair. It takes determination and dedication to be a just person. The Scriptures take justice a step further than fairness: justice is all about loving your neighbor.

- Temperance is about balance in your life. You know that stress, greed, or sickness comes from too much of a good thing. The pleasures in life must be balanced with moderation. The virtue of temperance is about self-control in all areas of our life.

- Fortitude is the moral virtue that strengthens us to overcome obstacles to living morally. It is easy to be good when we have no direct temptation in our life. When you are not feeling the ecstasy of being in love, the Church's teaching on premarital sex makes perfect sense. If you are not angry, nonviolence is a worthy ideal. But when you are in the heat of any moment, whether it is sexual passion or anger or some other strong feeling, fortitude gives you strength to overcome the temptation.

- Human virtues are a source of energy for choosing good moral actions. But faith, hope, and love—the theological virtues—are the source of energy for perfecting our relationships with God and neighbor. *Theological* means "the study of God." These virtues are theological because in accepting them and using them, we are drawn into deeper knowledge of and relationship with the Holy Trinity. Faith, hope, and love flow from God and back to God, providing an eternal power source of divine energy.

- Faith is belief in God. It is both a gift and a response. Faith is the gift of God inviting us to believe in him, never forcing the issue. Faith is also our response—we accept or reject the offer.

- Hope in God is closely connected to our faith. Hope enables us to keep our eye on the prize of heaven and eternal life. It inspires us in this life, helping us to overcome discouragement. Hope working together with faith and love gives us confidence to live the higher purpose of our life.

- And then there is love, also called charity. This is the greatest of all the theological virtues. Love is the virtue that gives life to the commandment to love God above all things, and our neighbor as ourself. God is love, and love is God. More than a feeling—even though feelings of love are wonderful—love is an attitude. At times we must go beyond feelings, and will ourselves to love others. Love like this, like God, makes all things possible.

6. List the four cardinal virtues and the three theological virtues on newsprint. Invite the four groups to go through the list of risks inherent in their scenario and to determine which of these virtues might help them face the risks. Ask each group to list the needed virtues on a separate sheet of newsprint. If any gaps appear to you, make suggestions.

7. The next task is to develop a plan for each scenario group to connect with some of these virtues before the members go out for the evening. Each group should identify a number of ways the scenario group can work on the virtues before going out. For example, work on prudence by thinking or talking through how the evening is expected to unfold so they can avoid impulsive action by not being caught off guard. The group should come up with a practical application of each virtue needed for the evening and plan how to connect with each virtue before the evening's activities get underway. Give the groups about 10 minutes for this activity.

8. Invite each of the four groups to share its scenario with all the participants, including what the risks are and how the virtues become a reality in life before the scenario begins.

9. Close with a few questions about how these suggestions can be put into practice in their daily life. Finally, be sure to note that the content of this session was drawn from chapter 30 of the *CFH*. Encourage the participants to read and review it in the next few days.

JournalACTIVITIES

◆ Pick one of the cardinal virtues that you would like to work on. Make a plan for practicing this virtue intentionally for one week. Check yourself at the end of the week to see how your plan made a difference. (*CFH*, p. 301)

◆ Reflect on a time when you needed forgiveness from someone. How hard was it to ask for forgiveness? How did you feel about being forgiven—or not forgiven? How hard is it for you to extend forgiveness to others? (*CFH*, p. 301)

◆ Which virtue is the hardest one for you to cultivate? Which one do you think you need the most? What blocks you from developing this virtue? Can you do something to remove the barrier?

Familyconnections

◆ Invite the participants to ask their parents and grandparents which virtue they most needed to cultivate as parents. Which virtue did they most need at work? Which virtue do they think they still need to work on?

◆ Invite families to start a grace box. They begin by spending a little time remembering graced moments—times when they are in touch with and nourished by God's love in family life. Examples might include a moment of reconciliation in the family, a quiet time appreciating a beautiful sunset as a family, or an unexpected act of kind-ness from a family member. Write a brief description of each moment on a slip of paper, and put those slips of paper in a box. Whoev-er in the family is in need of a little grace can pull one out. Every once in a while, add a new set of graced moments to the box.

◆ Invite families to brain-storm ways they can be instruments of grace in the lives of others. A family service project or a family justice project can be an opportunity to bond and to allow this love to be a gift to others.

Session Extensions

Labyrinth of Grace and Forgiveness (15 minutes)

Preparation

• Gather the following items:
  ❑ colored pens or pencils
  ❑ copies of handout 22, "My Labyrinth of Grace and Forgiveness" (or blank paper if you decide to have the participants draw a labyrinth), one for each participant
  ❑ newsprint
  ❑ markers

• If you decide to have the participants draw a labyrinth rather than use handout 22, review the instructions on how to draw a seven-circle labyrinth (on resource 6, "How to Draw a Labyrinth"). Practice drawing one a few times. Be prepared to demonstrate on a sheet of newsprint how to draw a labyrinth. Before beginning this session, prepare through step 3 of resource 4 the sheet that you are going to use for the demonstration.

1. Conduct a brief presentation on forgiveness and grace, using the bullet points below, which are taken from pages 298–301 of *The Catholic Faith Handbook for Youth (CFH):*

• A popular bumper sticker says, "Christians are not perfect, just forgiven." The question of forgiveness is important, because despite the fact that we are made in God's image and likeness, despite all the gifts that God has given us to follow his Law, we still sin.

• But the Gospel message, the good news (*Gospel* means "good news"), is that God is always ready to forgive us! All we need to do is turn to him in true sorrow and repentance and our sins are wiped away; we are free to begin again. There is no sin that can separate us from God's love and forgiveness.

• Grace happens. And it is amazing. We don't do anything to get grace. The most general definition of grace is that God is communicating to us at every moment of our existence.

• We can locate God's [grace] in multiple ways: stopping to give praise for all creation; being more aware of God's presence as we go about the routine of our daily life; prayer, worship, and the sacraments, of course, are guaranteed ways to experience God's grace. But we also experience grace through forgiveness. Through our Baptism and through the sacra-ment of Penance and Reconciliation, the Holy Spirit gives us sanctifying grace to heal our wounded soul and make us whole—and make us holy—again.

2. Distribute handout 22 (or blank paper) to the participants. Explain that they will use the pen or pencil to trace their way through the labyrinth. Guide them in the process with instructions similar to the following:

- This labyrinth serves as a metaphor for a lifelong journey of grace and forgiveness. We will journey slowly, the way sacred pilgrims once journeyed. In other words, this is not like a maze in a childhood activity book; the point is to go only as fast as I direct you, not to reach the center as quickly as possible. Please do not go any faster than I guide you.

- When I announce that we are getting to a turn, I mean that we are getting to one of these spots [indicate the turns on the labyrinth on the newsprint]. Do not make a turn until I talk about it. These turns are the focus of our reflection. If you wish to make a little note at each turn to remind you how you felt there, you are free to do so.

- People have used the labyrinth image and design in many ways for spiritual growth. Today we are going to use this labyrinth to reflect on the twists and turns of our lives.

- We begin this journey created in the image and likeness of God, and thus we are capable of knowing God and freely returning God's love. We enter the labyrinth at the bottom.

- We rapidly reach a turn in the labyrinth, which represents original sin. Original sin is the sin by which the first humans disobeyed God, resulting in separation from God; also, the state of human nature that affects every person now born into the world (*CFH,* p. 419). As we now trace through this first outer curve, we think about what it means to be born with original sin.

- In time we reach another turn, which represents the gift of grace and forgiveness that we receive at Baptism. We travel along this part of the path in the glow of this event, supported by the grace of the Holy Spirit.

- Eventually, though, we come to another turn, which symbolizes a time when we choose to do wrong in some way.

- At the next turn, we encounter the sacrament of Penance, or Reconciliation. Through this sacrament we experience a sign of God's forgiveness. The sanctifying grace of the Holy Spirit carries us along again for some time.

- Ever struggling with our human frailty, we come to another turn, and again we choose sin. We are older now and face more temptations.

- But this time things look brighter. We come to the next turn quickly, and we think that perhaps we have this sin thing beaten. We choose to receive the sacrament of Reconciliation soon after sinning. We might feel more empowered in the world. We might be thinking that with this sacrament, we can ward off sin. We might even begin to notice that God's grace is all around us if we pay attention to it.

- But suddenly, another turn appears, and we sin again. It is surprising how easy it is to fall into sin. The path we travel in sin might seem longer than the last one in a state of grace. But at this point, even if we are habitually doing wrong, we are on the lookout for grace, and we know one sure source of it, the sacrament of Penance, or Reconciliation.

- Something happens to break the habit of wrongs, and we come to another turn that offers forgiveness and grace. This turn into grace brings us to the center of the journey, to the present moment. Here we can rest in the reminder of God's grace.

- Resting in the center of this labyrinthine journey, we know that we eventually have to turn around and enter the twists and turns of life again. We might fear the possibility that we will sin again, but we know that we can look for grace and that God's forgiveness is always available to us.

- Rather than tracing our future on this labyrinth, we lift the pen and return our attention to the room. The metaphor of the labyrinth gives us hope when we are experiencing dark moments. Reconciliation and grace might be just around the corner.

Theological Virtues (20 minutes)

Preparation

- Gather the following items:
  - ❏ paper
  - ❏ markers
  - ❏ tape
  - ❏ newsprint
  - ❏ arts and crafts supplies

1. Conduct a brief presentation on the theological virtues, using the bullet points below, which are taken from pages 297–298 of *The Catholic Faith Handbook for Youth (CFH)*:

- Human virtues are a source of energy for choosing good moral actions. But faith, hope, and love—the theological virtues—are the source of energy for perfecting our relationships with God and neighbor. *Theological* means "the study of God." These virtues are theological because in accepting them and using them, we are drawn into deeper knowledge of and relationship with the Holy Trinity. Faith, hope, and love flow from God and back to God, providing an eternal power source of divine energy.

- Faith is belief in God. It is both a gift and a response. Faith is the gift of God inviting us to believe in him, never forcing the issue. Faith is also our response—we accept or reject the offer.

- Hope in God is closely connected to our faith. Hope enables us to keep our eye on the prize of heaven and eternal life. It inspires us in this life, helping us to overcome discouragement. Hope working together with faith and love gives us confidence to live the higher purpose of our life.
- And then there is love, also called charity. This is the greatest of all the theological virtues. Love is the virtue that gives life to the commandment to love God above all things, and our neighbor as ourself. God is love, and love is God. More than a feeling—even though feelings of love are wonderful—love is an attitude. At times we must go beyond feelings, and will ourselves to love others. Love like this, like God, makes all things possible.

2. Invite the participants to close their eyes and to picture one of the three theological virtues that you just spoke about. Ask them to get a clear picture of what that virtue looks like and how they would describe it to someone.

3. While they still have their eyes closed and are picturing one of the theological virtues, tell them that in a moment you are going to invite them to create something that represents the virtue they pictured. Share the following directions with them:

- They are free to develop whatever they would like as an artistic representation of the virtue.
- They can use the supplies you have provided to make a picture, sculpture, poem, story, song, or whatever else they choose.
- They are to do the activity alone and not to speak during the time everyone is working on this activity.

4. Once you have given these directions, tell the participants to open their eyes and begin creating their artistic interpretation of one of the theological virtues. Remind them to do this activity alone and in silence. Give them about 10 minutes to work on their images.

5. While the participants work on this activity, walk around and offer help wherever possible. To encourage the silence, you can play soft instrumental music in the background.

6. Call the group together, and invite the participants to share their images with the group.

7. To wrap up the activity, explain to the group that virtues are real. When we look at them in concrete ways, rather than just as ideas, we can more easily see how they fit into our life.

Spirit & Song
connections

◆ "Strength for the Journey," by Michael John Poirier

◆ "Prayer of Saint Francis/Oración de San Francisco," by Sebastian Temple

◆ "Hope to Carry On," by Rich Mullins

Inviting Virtue (10 minutes)

Preparation

• Clear a space large enough so the group can form a wide circle. Set up a tape player or a CD player.

• Choose a song from the *Spirit & Song* Connections or an alternative that reflects the theme of inviting virtue.

1. Ask the participants to stand in a circle facing outward and away from one another. To form the circle, ask the participants to join hands and expand the circle as far as their arms will reach. Before they release their hands, ask them to notice how broad and open the area around their heart is when their arms are stretched back like this. Invite them to drop their arms while still keeping the open posture around their heart.

2. Explain that you are going to read a series of reflection questions, followed by a prayer. Encourage the participants to be open to the prayer experience. Because they are not going to be asked to share their responses, they can be as honest as possible.

3. Lead the following prayer, which is based on the article "Prayer for a Virtuous Life," on page 297 of *The Catholic Faith Handbook for Youth.* Begin by reading the first reflection below. Allow several moments for reflection before you read the accompanying prayer. After the prayer, read the next reflection and prayer, and so on, until you complete all four reflections and prayers. Invite the participants to respond aloud to each prayer by saying, "God, I open my heart."

• **Reflection:** Think about what you most crave, what you want more of no matter how much you get.

• **Prayer:** Good and gracious God, when I feel the lure of excess and crave too much of a good thing, help me to develop temperance, the self-control that gives my life balance and wholeness.

• **Reflection:** Think of the thing you are most likely to do on impulse, the behavior that is most challenging for you to stop and think about before doing it.

• **Prayer:** Good and gracious God, when I feel driven to act on impulse, give me prudence, the wisdom to stop and think before I act.

- **Reflection:** Think about one way you get wrapped up in your own worries and desires.
- **Prayer:** Good and gracious God, when I find that I am preoccupied with myself, my own wants and worries, help me to see others with eyes of compassion and reach out to them with loving justice.
- **Reflection:** Think about one way you are tempted not to live morally, one way you are tempted to move away from God.
- **Prayer:** Good and gracious God, when I face obstacles to living morally that tempt me to move away from you, give me fortitude, the courage to overcome the temptation. Amen.

   4. Conclude the prayer by playing one of the songs listed under *Spirit & Song* Connections or an alternative that reflects the theme of inviting virtue.

Options and Actions

- **Virtues at work.** Have the participants ask their employer, or someone they know who is an employer, what virtues he or she looks for in a good employee. Have them ask their parents what virtues they think are most important at their workplace. Encourage the participants to develop a plan to cultivate some of these virtues in their own life so that when they apply for a job, they will be able to claim these virtues as their own.
- **Closer to God.** Invite the participants to identify an event or a moment in their life when they experienced faith, hope, or charity. Invite them to acknowledge this gift of virtue by writing to one or more of the people who have been instruments of that virtue. The letter can serve as a thank-you note for helping them get closer to God.
- **Forgiving others.** Invite the participants to look in the newspaper for an article about someone who has done something wrong or a story in which someone asks for forgiveness. Each week we read about such situations, ranging from someone who committed a crime to an athlete who missed a winning shot to a celebrity who did something that offended people. What do you think caused this person to ask for forgiveness? What would forgiveness for this person look like?

- **Grace and good works.** Many young people have heard someone say, "You'll earn a spot in heaven for that!" to affirm the young person for doing something positive. Ask the participants whether anyone has ever suggested that they can earn their way into heaven. Then have the group read the article "Grace and Works," on page 301 of *The Catholic Faith Handbook for Youth.* Ask them to discuss how this article changes their thinking, if at all, about the way they will approach doing good works in the future.

The Moral Life

This session covers pages 294–301 of *The Catholic Faith Handbook for Youth*. For further exploration, check out paragraph numbers 1803–1829, 1833–1844, and 1987–2029 of the *Catechism of the Catholic Church*.

Session Summary

- In the moral life, our heart tells us we want to learn to dance the right way, God's way. We have to use our head to learn the meaning of the commandments, which are the basic steps. We listen to the Beatitudes, which are the music that makes the steps come alive. But to best practice the moral life, we have to tap into the gifts God has placed within each one of us: the virtues, forgiveness, and grace.

- Virtues harness the good energy within us. They are habits that we develop over time to help us make good decisions. Like mastering skills in any sport, virtues capitalize on the abilities God has already placed within us.

- When virtues become natural to us, we don't always have to think about the mechanics of moral decision-making.

- There are two kinds of virtues—cardinal virtues and theological virtues. The cardinal virtues come with being human, regardless of religious belief. Jesus was a model for living the four virtues of prudence, justice, temperance, and fortitude. As you develop these four virtues in your life, you become a person of moral character. To have character means that you do the right thing, even under difficult circumstances.

- Prudence is the opposite of being impulsive. Acting impulsively is okay when you are two years old. It may even be appropriate in certain settings that call for creativity or spontaneity. But making moral decisions impulsively can get you into trouble. Prudence requires that you approach moral problems with a degree of caution. Also called wise judgment, prudence relies heavily on our reason. Prudence helps you to stop and think before you act.

- Justice is the virtue concerned with giving both God and neighbor what is their due. It is the habit of thinking about the needs of others as much as your own needs, and acting on what you know to be fair. It takes determination and dedication to be a just person. The Scriptures take justice a step further than fairness: justice is all about loving your neighbor.

- Temperance is about balance in your life. You know that stress, greed, or sickness comes from too much of a good thing. The pleasures in life must be balanced with moderation. The virtue of temperance is about self-control in all areas of our life.

- Fortitude is the moral virtue that strengthens us to overcome obstacles to living morally. It is easy to be good when we have no direct temptation in our life. When you are not feeling the ecstasy of being in love, the Church's teaching on premarital sex makes perfect sense. If you are not angry, nonviolence is a worthy ideal. But when you are in the heat of any moment, whether it is sexual passion or anger or some other strong feeling, fortitude gives you strength to overcome the temptation.

- Human virtues are a source of energy for choosing good moral actions. But faith, hope, and love—the theological virtues—are the source of energy for perfecting our relationships with God and neighbor. *Theological* means "the study of God." These virtues are theological because in accepting them and using them, we are drawn into deeper knowledge of and relationship with the Holy Trinity. Faith, hope, and love flow from God and back to God, providing an eternal power source of divine energy.

- Faith is belief in God. It is both a gift and a response. Faith is the gift of God inviting us to believe in him, never forcing the issue. Faith is also our response—we accept or reject the offer.

- Hope in God is closely connected to our faith. Hope enables us to keep our eye on the prize of heaven and eternal life. It inspires us in this life, helping us to overcome discouragement. Hope working together with faith and love gives us confidence to live the higher purpose of our life.

- And then there is love, also called charity. This is the greatest of all the theological virtues. Love is the virtue that gives life to the commandment to love God above all things, and our neighbor as ourself. God is love, and love is God. More than a feeling—even though feelings of love are wonderful—love is an attitude. At times we must go beyond feelings, and will ourselves to love others. Love like this, like God, makes all things possible.

- A popular bumper sticker says, "Christians are not perfect, just forgiven." The question of forgiveness is important, because despite the fact that we are made in God's image and likeness, despite all the gifts that God has given us to follow his Law, we still sin.

- But the Gospel message, the good news (*Gospel* means "good news"), is that God is always ready to forgive us! All we need to do is turn to him in true sorrow and repentance and our sins are wiped away, we are free to begin again. There is no sin that can separate us from God's love and forgiveness.

- Grace happens. And it is amazing. We don't do anything to get grace. The most general definition of grace is that God is communicating to us at every moment of our existence.
- We can locate God's [grace] in multiple ways: stopping to give praise for all creation; being more aware of God's presence as we go about the routine of our daily life; prayer, worship, and the sacraments, of course, are guaranteed ways to experience God's grace. But we also experience grace through forgiveness. Through our Baptism and through the sacrament of Penance and Reconciliation, the Holy Spirit gives us sanctifying grace to heal our wounded soul and make us whole—and make us holy—again.

(All summary points are taken from *The Catholic Faith Handbook for Youth,* by Brian Singer-Towns et al. [Winona, MN: Saint Mary's Press, 2004], pages 295–301. Copyright © 2004 by Saint Mary's Press. All rights reserved.)

Talk Points

- What virtues have you developed with the help of your family without even realizing it until recently?
- Think about the saints you have heard of, or look at a couple of the "Saintly Profiles" in *The Catholic Faith Handbook for Youth*. Do you presume that these people were born with more capacity for virtue than anyone else, or do you think they worked at developing the virtues as hard as you have to do?
- Where in your life could you use some temperance?

Virtue-al Reality

A mall on a Friday night. A group of friends is going to the mall to shop, hang out, eat, talk, and flirt. One friend wants a leather jacket that is on display in a new shop. Another person wants to tell a story about two people at school. One shop has the best cookies on the planet. A certain cute new kid will probably be at the mall. What moral dilemmas might arise in this scenario?

A party with high school students from the area. A group of friends is going to a party to talk, laugh, hang out, flirt, and have fun. This week the party is at the home of a new kid whose parents are away and who, you heard, have a big liquor cabinet. You also heard rumors that the new kid does drugs on the weekend. In addition, someone you like is going to be there who, you heard, might be breaking up with someone after dating for the past three months. What moral dilemmas might arise in this scenario?

A school sporting event. A group of friends is going to a school sporting event to enjoy the game, cheer for their team, give the other team a hard time, talk, laugh, hang out, and get something to eat afterward. The other team is the big school rival, and you heard that they were planning a prank. A fight occurred the last time the two schools played each other. A bunch of really good looking kids go to the other school. After the last game, a contest took place to see who could eat the most pizza. Tradition calls for toilet-papering the yard of the MVP's home. What moral dilemmas might arise in this scenario?

A sci-fi film at the local cinema. A group of friends is going to see the latest science-fiction film at the local cinema. Following the movie, one of the girls in the group will drive everyone back to her house because her parents are gone for the evening. The plans for later in the evening are to sit around talking, eating, and playing the latest video games. One friend shares that he has been cooking up something in his chemistry lab for the group to try—he promises that it is legal. What moral dilemmas might arise in this scenario?

How to Draw a Labyrinth

1. Make a Greek cross on the page by drawing two lines of equal length that intersect in the center.
2. In each quadrant, a short distance from the original intersection, draw two short, intersecting lines to form a 90-degree angle; these two arms, which are parallel to two of the lines of the original intersection, form two sides of an imaginary square.
3. Mark a dot at what would be the outermost corner of this imaginary square.
4. Beginning at the top of the Greek cross that you made in step 1, draw an arc to the top of the next parallel line to the right (that is, to the top of the line that you drew in step 3).
5. Beginning at the top of the vertical line to the left of your first arc (the one that you drew in step 4), draw another arc over and above that first arc, ending at the dot that is to the right of your first arc.
6–11. Each of these steps involves drawing an arc that begins one line or one dot to the left of the previous arc and ends on one line or one dot to the right of the previous arc.

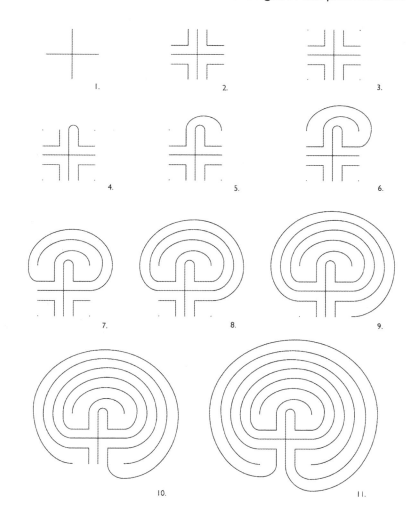

My Labyrinth
of Grace and Forgiveness

Acknowledgments

The scriptural quotations contained herein are from the New Revised Standard Version of the Bible, Catholic Edition. Copyright © 1993 and 1989 by the Division of Christian Education of the National Council of the Churches of Christ in the United States of America. All rights reserved.

The material labeled *CFH* or *Catholic Faith Handbook* is from *The Catholic Faith Handbook for Youth,* by Brian Singer-Towns et al. (Winona, MN: Saint Mary's Press, 2004). Copyright © 2004 by Saint Mary's Press. All rights reserved.

The material labeled *CYB* or *Catholic Youth Bible* is from *The Catholic Youth Bible,* first edition (Winona, MN: Saint Mary's Press, 2000). Copyright © 2000 by Saint Mary's Press. All rights reserved.

The material labeled *CCC* or *Catechism* is from the English translation of the *Catechism of the Catholic Church* for use in the United States of America. Copyright © 1994 by the United States Catholic Conference, Inc.—Libreria Editrice Vaticana. Used with permission.

The information about the goals and vision for ministry with adolescents on page 7 is from *Renewing the Vision: A Framework for Catholic Youth Ministry,* by the United States Conference of Catholic Bishops' (USCCB) Department of Education (Washington, DC: USCCB, 1997), pages 1–2. Copyright © 1997 by the USCCB, Inc. All rights reserved.

The excerpt about man's love for the Creator on page 21 is quoted from Pope John Paul II's *Pastoral Constitution on the Church in the Modern World* (*Gaudium et Spes,* 1965), number 12, at *www.vatican.va/archive/ hist_councils/ii_vatican_council/documents/vat-ii_cons_19651207_gaudium-et-spes_en.html,* accessed March 8, 2004.

The excerpt from Pope John Paul II's *Dilecti Amici* on page 21, quoted in *The Catholic Faith Handbook for Youth,* page 209, is reprinted by permission of *L'Osservatore Romano.*

The activity on pages 22–23, the option on page 26, and handout 3 are adapted from *Called to Live the Gospel,* by Marilyn Kielbasa (Winona, MN: Saint Mary's Press, 2000), pages 23–24, 24, and 30, respectively. Copyright © 2000 by Saint Mary's Press. All rights reserved.

The activity on pages 34–35 is adapted from the activity "We Can Do That Too! Simulations," by Ten Days for Global Justice, Canada, at the Church World Service Web page, *www.churchworldservice.org/wecantoo/ sim1.html,* accessed March 8, 2004. Used with permission of Tom Hampson.

The quote on page 36 is by Ruth Smeltzer, as quoted at the Great Quotations Web page, *www.cyber-nation.com/victory/quotations/authors/ quotes_smeltzer_ruth.html,* accessed March 8, 2004. Copyright © 1999 by Cyber Nation International, Inc.

The family discussion suggestion on handout 4 is adapted from "Balancing Rights and Responsibilities," in *Justice: Building God's Reign,* by Karen Emmerich (Winona, MN: Saint Mary's Press, 1997), page 37. Copyright © 1997 by Saint Mary's Press. All rights reserved.

The poem on handout 6 comes from "#89," in *A Far Rockaway of the Heart,* by Lawrence Ferlinghetti (New York: New Directions, 1997), page 107. Copyright © 1997 by Lawrence Ferlinghetti. Used with permission of New Directions Publishing Corp.

The activity on pages 51–52 is adapted from *Deciding as a Christian,* by Brian Singer-Towns (Winona, MN: Saint Mary's Press, 1996), page 22. Copyright © 1996 by Saint Mary's Press. All rights reserved.

Steps 1 and 2 of the activity on page 60 are adapted from "Idle Idols," in *High School Talksheets: Psalms and Proverbs—Updated!* by Rick Bundschuh and Tom Finley (Grand Rapids, MI: Youth Specialties, 2001), page 46. Copyright © 2001 by Youth Specialties. Used with permission of Zondervan.

The quote by Leo Tolstoy on page 60 is from *That the World May Believe,* by Hans Küng (New York: Sheed and Ward, 1963), page 143. Copyright © 1963 by Sheed and Ward. Used with permission.

The activities on pages 64–66, 144–145, and 145–146, are adapted from *Teaching Activities Manual for "The Catholic Youth Bible,"* by Christine Schmertz Navarro et al. (Winona, MN: Saint Mary's Press, 2000), pages 39, 307–308, and 314–315. Copyright © 2000 by Saint Mary's Press. All rights reserved.

The prayer on resource 2 is adapted from the Pray It™ article "A Prayer for Friends," John 18:6, in *The Catholic Youth Bible,* first edition (Winona, MN: Saint Mary's Press, 2000). Copyright © 2000 by Saint Mary's Press. All rights reserved.

The activity on pages 91–93 and handout 13 is adapted from "It's Wrong No Matter Who Does It," in *Straight from the Heart and Other Stories,* by Lisa Calderone-Stewart and Ed Kunzman (Winona, MN: Saint Mary's Press, 1999), pages 36–40. Copyright © 1999 by Saint Mary's Press. All rights reserved.

The story of Dorothy Day on page 94 is adapted from "Life," in *Way to Live: Christian Practices for Teens, Leader's Guide,* by Dorothy C. Bass and Don C. Richter (Nashville, TN: Upper Room Books, 2002), page 14. Copyright © 2002 by Dorothy C. Bass and Don C. Richter. Adapted with permission of Upper Room Books.

The option "Lifesavers" on page 97 is adapted from *Sharing the Sunday Scriptures with Youth: Cycle C,* by Maryann Hakowski, (Winona, MN: Saint Mary's Press, 1997), page 93. Copyright © 1997 by Saint Mary's Press. All rights reserved.

The activity on pages 111–112 is from *Sexuality: Challenges and Choices,* by Michael Theisen (Winona, MN: Saint Mary's Press, 1996), page 49. Copyright © 1996 by Saint Mary's Press. All rights reserved.

The option "Treasure Sexuality" on page 113 is adapted from *Scripture Walk Senior High: Discipleship,* by Nora Bradbury-Haehl (Winona, MN: Saint Mary's Press, 2000), page 74. Copyright © 2000 by Saint Mary's Press. All rights reserved.

The excerpt by Harriet G. Lerner on page 145 is found in *Openings: Quotations on Spirituality in Everyday Life,* compiled by Shelley Tucker (Seattle, WA: Whiteaker Press, 1997), page 19. Copyright © 1997 by Shelley Tucker. Used with permission.

The prayer on resource 5 is quoted from *Seasons of Your Heart: Prayers and Reflections,* by Macrina Wiederkehr (New York: HarperCollins, 1991), pages 99–100. Copyright © 1991 by Macrina Wiederkehr. All rights reserved. Used with permission of HarperCollins Publishers, Inc.

To view copyright terms and conditions for Internet materials cited here, log on to the home pages for the referenced Web sites.

During this book's preparation, all citations, facts, figures, names, addresses, telephone numbers, Internet URLs, and other pieces of information cited within were verified for accuracy. The authors and Saint Mary's Press staff have made every attempt to reference current and valid sources, but we cannot guarantee the content of any source, and we are not responsible for any changes that may have occurred since our verification. If you find an error in, or have a question or concern about, any of the information or sources listed within, please contact Saint Mary's Press.

Endnotes Cited in Quotations from the *Catechism of the Catholic Church*

Chapter 1
1. Cf. *Gaudium et spes* 12 § 1 1; 24 § 3; 39 § 1.

Handout 5
1. Cf. *Gaudium et spes* 26 § 2.

Chapter 3
1. St. Thomas Aquinas, *Dec. præc.* I.

Handout 7
1. St. Thomas Aquinas, *Dec. præc.* I.

Handout 12
1. John Paul II, *Evangelium vitae* 56.